JUST *Justly Justice*!

"Social Justice," "Racial Justice," "Human Rights"…

done!

Kevin McGary

JUST Justly Justice!

ISBN: 978-0-9876782-6-3

When individuals are quoted, unless explicitly stated, the author does not intend to endorse those individuals or any of their *other* writings, positions, lifestyles or beliefs.

Unless noted, all ***emphasis*** in quotes were added by the author.

Rather than use awkward phrasing, the author has chosen to use the generic mankind, men, man, his or he to indicate both genders and has chosen to violate the plural rules, using "their" instead of "his or her" where appropriate.

Contact the author at kevin@fdfca.org

PREFACE

All hearts innately yearn for justice! Dr. Martin Luther King appropriately confirms, “injustice anywhere is a threat to justice everywhere.”

God’s divine nature has infused all men with a fundamental desire for justice. From the beginning of mankind and in any culture or society, justice is recognized as a unifying principle. While it is universally heralded , it also happens to be one of those terms that is relatively hard to define. If we asked a million people to define it, we would invariably have a million definitions on a basic theme; but, a definitive meaning would still certainly elude us.

If we were to ask some of the most notoriously evil and demented minds in human history (Hitler, Stalin, Mao, Lenin, etc.), they would all assert that their actions were sincere “justice” movements. They would insist that they had to take definitive actions to bring about “fairness” and eliminate oppressors and impending tyranny. This is the crux of the problem! Simply, justice has tended to be a matter of perspective. And, as perspective is subjective, so has the execution and perversion of justice tended to be.

Based on thousands of conversations shared during hundreds of workshops, forums and speaking engagements, I contend there is a quantifiable definition of justice that can be boiled down and crystallized into a central culminating truth. Needless to say, going- forward terms like “fairness” must be resoundingly rejected, as its lack of definable qualities and measurement is unacceptable.

The world needs clarity and an actual definition that can produce uncompromising unity and focus, which may generate momentum in the quest for justice. While fairness (and other terms like it) seems to connote a modicum of justice, its roots and foundations are actually demonic (more on this later) and do not represent measureable and irreproachable truth.

Too much time has passed, too many deaths have occurred, and too many justice movements have failed! Our desperate times have created a real urgency for justice, as our very hearts and souls ache to the point we are ready align, depend and defend it! Now is the time, this is the place, and is the season for a renewed and reinvigorated justice.

Heretofore, we have bungled the issue of justice because of its variances and obscurities that accompany it. We must move from having simplistic justice advocacy on the peripheral, to adopting a fervent lifestyle in complete alignment with the embodiment of real justice. By the end of this book we will find that the subject of justice can be made coherent and can be "*done*"; additionally, we will confirm that just "justly justice" is the only distinction to suffice in our overarching commitment to justice.

With sincerest gratitude, I thank you in advance for your courage to read this book, and desire for and commitment to real justice. Your participation with this topic will help produce a positive transformation in America, and allow us all to dutifully transition to justly justice … Indeed!

"Where justice is denied, where poverty is enforced, where ignorance prevails, and where any one class is made to feel that society is in an organized conspiracy to oppress, rob, and degrade them, neither persons nor property will be safe."

~ Honorable Frederick Douglass

Blessings from your brother and servant,

Kevin

INTRODUCTION

Do you stand for justice? Are you principled and righteous? Does your stance ensure fair and equal treatment for all mankind? What about your favorite political pundits and party? Do they truly stand for justice? How do you (or can you) know with absolute certainty that all your vested and endorsed people, parties or agencies are really committed to justice? These are some of the questions you will be able to definitively answer and confirm while reading this book.

This book is an action-plan designed to help confront and dismantle some of the most problematic issues that destroy societal advancement, trust and unity, and the individual's ability to experience freedom and human dignity. Since most of us who are committed to causes take actions purely based on a rudimentary understanding of "justice" (i.e., participate in marches, lead discussion/forums, support candidates and vote, etc.), it is vitally important to confirm exactly what it is. "Justly Justice" is a term that signifies a wholly righteous and Holy consistent form of justice that is (from any angle or perspective) beyond reproach. It is a term that is not tied to agenda, factions or political party. Conversely, it is strictly tied to truth and an indisputable righteousness. The goal is to discover whether indeed we can or will stand for this brand of justice in its purest, irrevocable and irreproachable form.

While this book is written for everyone, be forewarned. It is written for the courageous who are serious about the issue of justice! For some, it may appear to be scholarly and cerebral but this is purposeful and intentional so please bear with it. After the first two chapters, it will become more plainspoken and matter-of-fact. Recurrence and repetition are also used strategically throughout the book; this is also quite purposeful. Since we are attempting to shift well-entrenched traditions, mindsets and ideologies, a pattern of some degree of repetition is vital. I have no hesitancy in saying this book will produce truly transformative results for the entirety of U.S. culture and society if everyone reads it. You will find there is also special emphasis that has been incorporated to help all churches and denominations, synagogues, community leaders, and political leaders, to holistically connect and embrace their respective passions in the truest and irreproachable ways. Ill-defined or vague definitions for our respective justice causes, are what limits the capacity to achieve maximum results; the charter of this book is to finally put all vagaries to rest, which will allow actual quantifiable success!

Systemic poverty, human rights atrocities, basic undermining of social and racial justice, along with long histories of inequalities are some of the major issues talked about as plaguing our social and cultural interactions. Injustices of all sorts have always existed. Let's face it. As regrettable as it is, perpetuating injustices is an inescapable part of mankind's many imperfections and fallen nature; the good news is, we don't have to permanently succumb or be resigned to it. We will find that once we have the capacity to recognize and observe it, we can actually do something about it. Make no mistake, though. Doing something about it will require that we are ready, willing and able to do battle.

In order to win any battle, all warriors must thoroughly understand the mission, they need to possess clarity and perspective on the objective, and they must be able to coordinate actions in order to "rally the troops" while getting everyone in position to battle for a win. This is basic and fundamental to any battle. In order to effectively combat the many triggers and perturbations that threaten our success with achieving social justice, racial justice and human rights.

Due to a constant barrage of media reports projecting calamity of one sort or another, it seems we are perpetually in a battle for all humanity. Many battles we currently face revolve around combating some of the most pressing social and cultural issues of our lifetimes. Ironically, these battles are not new, as they seem to have preoccupied us for centuries (having morphed in one form or another); now, after evolving from relatively barbaric societies, through centuries of education and sophistication, these matters urgently deserve definitive solutions. This book will help illuminate issues related to our most complex and perplexing social problems used to perpetuate injustices and break them down to the simplest forms of their foundational element(s), so we can finally derive a method to end the scourge of atrocities and human suffering. This is indeed lofty, but if we have the courage to engage, comprehend, and act, we will be able to work together with new-found vigor.

As mentioned, special emphasis is given for all teachers and educators, Pastors and ministers, all political Parties/political leaders/pundits, and for all "special interest" and advocate organizations who purport sincerity in their unequivocal commitment in trying to deal with issues of injustice. While working with these factions, I find they are in need of better tools for grounding a commitment to their respective causes. It will (no doubt) culminate into an "aha" moment at some point during the reading; when this occurs, it is vitally important to redouble the rigor and press through this entire book because by the end we will have discovered new language and vernacular, and new ways to discuss and empower our respective constituencies. The goal is to permanently change the trajectory and momentum of gross injustices.

There's something in this for everybody, and especially the courageous. This book is specially written for the courageous! If you are a "social justice" advocate, you should gain new perspective. If you are a "racial justice" proponent, you will be greatly challenged about your commitment toward the incredible need for actual racial justice. If you are a Human Rights advocate (anywhere in the world) you will be faced with new realities about how to appropriately combat brazen evils in order to combat the pattern of human rights atrocities. If you are a Pastor, Priest or any type of Minister/Ministry, you will be theologically challenged to the extent your message and stance for Righteousness will become wholly consistent and beyond reproach.

A final note; while terms like social justice, racial justice and human rights are used throughout this book, please know these terms are being used to present a baseline and context for appropriately deconstructing meaning and producing coherent basis for observation and conversation. These terms, in their current social/cultural context, are not terms I wholly agree with as they may actually disempower the prudent and confound the wise, but please let it be known that if we are not careful, these very distinctions can be used to produce more death and destruction than they actually portend to help ease or cure. Gaining proper definition, understanding context, getting to the heart of the matters, and achieving wholly coherent and Holy consistent principles, we will thrive in assuring justly justice; for that reason, the book is organized in this exact chapter progression.

CONTENTS

Chapter One

DEFINE AND CONQUER

New frontier in the battle for justice

"Virtue cannot separate itself from reality without becoming a principle of evil."

~Albert Camus

We are perpetually in a battle for justice. While battle seems to characterize a military archetype, battle is indeed the correct term to use when discussing justice, as justice is always pursued in some form of conflict.

During times of conflict, a tried and true strategy involves dividing one's enemy in order to conquer it. In isolation, separated from tactical support and supply lines, the enemy becomes weakened and vulnerable. Furthermore, success in any battle requires a clear definition or understanding of its strategic significance and ultimate end-game scenario; this allows all participants a specific strategic definition of the battle and the respective end-game; this allows all participants to maximize use of their various assets (tools and capabilities) to ensure unity and victory. It has been proven, just the simple act of properly defining a battle (and respective end-game) provides exponential possibility for prevailing, when attempting to triumph in battles. The focus of this chapter is to properly characterize and acutely define the battle for justice so we can finally begin to conquer and prevail over injustices.

At some point in our lives, we have experienced being purposely lied to, misled and duped into believing something that is slightly incorrect or manifestly untrue. Unfortunately, many untruths pervade various movements. While many times they are not purposely posited, untruths can take on a life of their own and overwhelm the purity of the cause. Often this occurs because even the slightest manipulation of truth has the capacity to generate more interest and emotional investment from participants of movement. A case in point is, even if what we really believe about a movement is actually untrue (mostly or even just partially), our emotions are triggered, we emotionally invest, and our actions and intentions are keenly altered to strongly reflect our buy-in to the object (even if it's of deceit). When we ultimately find out we have been intentionally duped and misled, most react very strongly to such treachery and deceit as we realize we have invested our time, energies, and our heart and souls into believing something that was completely false from the start. After determined introspection as to why we were misled, we usually find there were obvious signs of something askew but we were blinded by a compelling, visceral narrative. This happens far too frequently within movements, so what we need is to have better methods of ferreting out truth before we invest.

Being swept into action keeps us wound up and busy, but does little more than that. To become more effective in solving the primary social and cultural issues of our day, there is great need to move beyond being emotionally outraged and stymied due to lack of actions; the most urgent need is to understand what it is (at its most base level) we are trying to accomplish and why. The reality is, most of what we think we understand and wholly identify with as injustices can be filtered down and crystallized into a very simple common denominator. If we can appropriately identify that single object (common denominator), we can finally begin to definitively work toward solving issues of injustice in a coordinated and strategic fashion. If we will pursue finally resolving objects of injustice, we should be preoccupied with the question, "is my cause truly 'just'?" The fact is, we all are short of time and resources. So if we don't want to waste our most precious resources of time and energies, how can we definitively confirm what is truly a just cause deserving of our investment?

For the most part, what has precluded coordinated and effective action in dealing with injustices is their relative obscurity. The lack of consistency in defining our object (in this case, social/racial and human rights injustices) precludes appropriately conveying and discerning the real focus with issues of injustice. While committing my life and resources to justice causes, I have found obscurity of the cause is often purposeful and strategic. Many times, those who have been empowered to lead the battle for bringing issues of injustice to light are the very ones whose sole or primary interest is to "profit" (either by gaining leadership and stature, or by garnering hard dollars/donations, etc.) and therefore see battling under the banner of nebulous and obscure distinctions, as a benefit rather than foe!

Obscurity can be quite a strategic weapon! The fact is, producing the emotional response of outrage and disgust has proven to provide powerful motivation; for those with singularly nefarious motivations like to get elected, to garner support for "pet" causes, to become a leader of a movement, to generate donations, etc., too often the goal is to find a motivator that propels people into action, rather than to acutely and precisely define and conquer a matter of outrage and injustice. With these types of individuals, the object of the task is to characterize and demonize in the most abstract, veiled and obscure way possible so the emotional response (i.e., collective outrage) overwhelms and supersedes the original object of scorn. It gets to a point where people's heightened emotions and sensitivities then become the drivers of the movement instead of the actual identified causes that were its prelude. Needless to say, this does not work to the advantage of the effectiveness of the movement; most times however, it works quite well to the personal advantage of the authors of the purported movement.

Labels define movements. Nebulous labels define inefficiency. To arrive at a point of which can be deemed as a readily definable, pure and irreproachable form of justice ("justly justice"), a level of study and intention must be invested in discerning the details of the respective cause. I realize it may be hard for some to fathom that anyone would or could take noble labels like "social justice," "racial justice" and "human rights" and use them as a ruse and rallying cry to just stir and foment emotions, but it does happen. Regrettably, too often this is precisely what is happening and will plague movements until we wise up to tactics and demand clarity. The goal is to ensure our best intentions and earnest heartstrings are not manipulated to prevent what we've seen occur throughout history.

There have been many good-hearted and well-intended people who, due to relative obscurity of their respective cause, unwittingly proved to be nothing more than useful dupes for some of the most notoriously evil people in world history. W.E.B. Dubois, writing in the National Guardian (1953), said, "Joseph Stalin was a great man; few other men of the 20th century approach his stature ... But also – and this was the highest proof of his greatness – he knew the common man, felt his problems, followed his fate." New York Times journalist, Walter Duranty, called Stalin "the greatest living statesman ... a quiet, unobtrusive man." Heralded writer and Nobel Prize recipient, George Bernard Shaw, expressed admiration for Mussolini, Hitler and Stalin. Many others, including some in the Obama administration (Ron Bloom and Anita Dunn) have praised, admired and lauded Mao and his "achievements." These are examples of purportedly learned men of noble history, and yet they became unwitting dupes lauding brazen evil. Wow! Consider that for a moment. If learned men of great stature can be horribly duped into believing manifest evil is "good" or honorable, what precludes us from being all the more grossly misled?

Noted historical figures, scholars, pioneers, and politicians have been grossly misled into thinking much more nobly of people (and their respective movements) than they deserved; in hindsight, it is quite clear these people were evil incarnate and deserved no praise! The question we should ask then is, "how could so many notable well-educated and purportedly well-informed people be so horribly misguided?" It is undeniable that under their banner of "the great purge," the Nazis forced many into slave labor, sent many millions into Gulags, and have been estimated to be responsible for the murder of over 20 million people. In all, Stalin and his successors murdered, or were otherwise responsible for the deaths of 62 million of their own people. Under the soaring rhetoric of the "great leap forward" (this sounds quite familiar), Mao and his successors were responsible for the deaths of approximately 90 million Chinese. We know the evil and quite notorious fascistic despot Hitler was responsible for the deaths of at least six million Jews, but after factoring in at least five million gypsies, Poles, Slavs, slave laborers, homosexuals, and victims of euthanasia, we can easily attribute over 20 million deaths to him. Over 100 million deaths have occurred as a result of the most heinous acts known to man! Contrary to the rhetoric of the day about how compassionate other forms of government are, all 100 million+ deaths have been precipitated at the hands of Fascists, Marxists, Communists and Socialists. How can so many of even the "elect" among us (scholars, politicians, etc.) be so horribly deceived as to laud and praise such notorious men? Blindness! We have been largely blinded, and the evil (while it was manifest) has been veiled and obscured.

How can tens of millions men, women and children be maimed and abused, and be forced to endure atrocities, and ultimately be put to death without the leaders being held accountable? Is it possible that the world can fall into a collective stupor and even today allow gross atrocities to occur right in front of us? The answer is yes! Through the use of flowery colorful language and vague distinctions, it is possible to obscure any atrocity while evoking complicity to the evil act itself. To be sure, we should recognize that while Hitler, Stalin, Mao and others perpetuated their brutal crimes against all humanity, there was a common theme amongst these demented men and the groups that supported them. National unity, rights for the workers, wealth redistribution, "democracy," inequality, and most notably "social justice" provided a platform upon which these demonically inspired men were able to carry out any evil scheme they wanted. Imagine that! The most notoriously evil people in the history of mankind used the exact same terms and distinctions being used today to characterize movements for justice! What we see happen was that people wholly supported, paid attention to, and rallied around the populist themes being touted; the underlying principles were veiled or purposely obscured and the worst of gross atrocities occurred right under their eyes. Energies and emotions were vested in a theme, not the abhorrent acts or actions that precipitated the theme. This is a most regrettable yet predictable outcome when obscurity is maintained.

When we connect the dots of history, a troubling but ever-clear and unmistakable pattern emerges about what happens when obscurity and vagaries are allowed to grow and fester. To circumvent misguided participation in movements or prevailing social/cultural agendas that may have been solely developed for purposes of tyranny, personal aggrandizement, or to just garner participation for inciting rallying cries based on pure emotion, there is need for clear and meaningful definition so we can accomplish transparency and accountability. Clear definition objectifies our cause, it helps focus our actions and attention, and it unifies. We need to define in order to conquer.

Unless we demand precise definitions of justice, history confirms it is not unrealistic that we may find ourselves unwittingly participating in the next genocide. This would go against our good intentions and very nature, while allowing others to take full advantage of our sensibilities and kindness. The fact is, most of us are not be able to confirm and define what Hitler and Stalin meant when they touted " justice" as their rallying cries to their respective citizenry. If we're completely honest with ourselves, we can't appropriately define what social justice means today. This is dangerous! The clearest method for observing whether something is indeed a legitimate crisis and worth our "investment" is to know that it can be always be clearly defined as such; the meaning of it would not change or morph into a varying narrative (irrespective of length time passed, culture, or place). For instance, Hitler's genocide against the Jews is something that stands out for all of humanity as a world tragedy for which we vow to "never forget." And yet, the procession of genocidal tyrants grows longer with each generation.

While some would attempt to dismiss the misuse and abuse of the term "social justice" as something that only occurred in yesteryears with dictators long gone, please know that even to this day Fidel Castro and his brother rally behind the label of "social justice" while exercising horrible tyranny and oppression against the Cuban people. Actually, even to this day most South American dictators use and hide behind the banner of social justice. This begs the question, is it possible that today, people can become so engrossed with pure emotion that brazen atrocities can again happen without notice or outrage? Can some of us become so gripped, blinded and swayed by soaring rhetoric making urgent claims about the need for "income equality," "marriage equality," "environmental justice" and etc. that we sorely miss the central point of the cause? Could it be that claims of "racial injustice" without any definition or clarity, can itself foment racial hatred toward others? Could it be that claims of social justice, without any firm or clarifying distinctions, can foment hatred and intolerance toward other people, organizations or political/Parties with alternate views? Could it be that while the U.S. purports to be the harbinger of freedoms and human rights, it can (at the same time) also wholly participate in and condone demonization, polarization and dehumanization of some of its own citizens? Can it be that while we individually listen and participate in the ever-polarized language, pledge allegiance to political ideology and participate in Balkanization throughout the world, we are living a life that epitomizes duplicity and abject hypocrisy? If we are honest with ourselves, we would say all of these are distinct possibilities! After historically confirming how easy it is to get swept up in fervor (like with Hitler when he stated, "as a Christian I have no duty to allow myself to be cheated, but I have the duty to be a fighter for truth and justice"), we should assert it is not only possible, it is highly probable.

As we pursue definition and clarity about the various issues surrounding basic injustice, we should keep a fundamental truth as paramount in our minds: all injustice is injustice! If we excuse and supplant one type of injustice for the sake of honoring and strongly identifying with another injustice, we are dutifully participating in a cycle of hypocritical nonsense. This undermines any commitment to personal integrity, and causes the loss of all creditability. There is urgent need to define and confirm our principled stance in order to prevent our own circuitous hypocrisy. Since social justice, racial justice and human rights are rather nebulous terms conspicuously vague, and seemingly veiled in their true meaning and intent, we should want to purposely and intently look deeper into their meanings and distinctions to determine if indeed they truly mean what we think (and hope) they mean. Now is the time to sort out these definitions.

Injustices (in general) are invariably just as difficult to define as love is. We've heard many define love as, "I know it when I see (or feel) it"; even as we arrive at this point in our cultural sophistication and history, most people can't quite define love. Social/racial justice and human rights are in many ways just as nebulous. Most people, including even the "leaders" of these movements, can't quite define their respective cause. But, we must ask ourselves, why? These "justice" terms have been around for over 100 years. How can people be triggered and provoked into collective outrage with a mere mention of "injustice," but not be able to accurately define the object of our frustration? Do our emotions somehow play into a larger strategy to keep us so occupied with the emotion that we miss the point? If so, what is the point?

I have been speaking and conducting workshops with clergy and to other rather large political audiences for several years. After engaging countless thousands of people, I still haven't heard a good concise answer as to what clearly defines social justice. As we have already noted, this is problematic. Likewise, I have not been able to arrive at concise definitions that would appropriately characterize racial justice or human rights either. What's notable is, while I get the predictable vagaries that come when people try to answer and appropriately define something when put on the spot, there does seem to be a common thread and a baseline connection between all of these distinctions. Regrettably, the common thread I have uncovered is veiled in purposeful and strategic obscurity (more on this later).

We already noted why and how obscurity could be used as a powerful tool and motivator for "justice" causes. Instead of specifically and precisely defining a cause, obscurity coupled with lofty rhetoric can be used to dupe and deploy the masses.

Nothing levels the playing field of life better than sanitizing it with the light of truth. When we come to know and distinguish the truth, the truth will indeed set us free. This means we must come to the central point of our respective cause. The fact is, if we come to know and understand the central point of injustices, we will be able to define it. And if we can define, we can begin to solve. As we begin to solve, we can truly commit our lives to the solution. If we commit our lives to solving injustice, we will ultimately triumph in ending it! The point is, we must get to the "it."

In this chapter we have begun to see a fundamental lack of definition, and some of the reprehensible consequences that result; this only confirms, there is desperate need for clarity. The sad truth is, if we can't define the "it" to which we have (in some cases) pledged our life goals and resources, we are wholly unmoored and drifting toward an unspecified target. We must now come to know, understand and appropriately define the "it" into which we have (likely) already invested some degree of our time and resources. A generically defined justice should now no longer be acceptable since it is vague and therefore obviously beyond reproach. It has been already established and confirmed, the worst genocidal dictators in history (and their respective atrocities) were precipitated while using justice terms. We don't want their form of justice; we want what can only be defined as justly justice! Only a deeper and more intense look at definitions and context will help find what can only be construed as "justly justice."

Chapter Two

GETTING TO THE POINT

The crux of the matter, is the matter

> *"For every ten people who are clipping at the branches of evil, you're lucky to find one who's hacking at the roots."*
>
> *~Henry David Thoreau*

What has already been established that the last thing people who are sincere about helping solve and cure injustices would want is to be duped into participating in someone's evil schemes (like the minions who followed Hitler, Mao, Stalin, etc.). Lenin referred to people who were willingly ignorant yet useful for his purposes, as "useful idiots." While it is harsh and offensive, it does show the level of contempt leaders of movements have for the grossly misinformed. Certainly we do not want to participate in (or unwittingly become dupes for) the empowerment of savvy marketeers who perpetuate tyranny and evil; we would like to believe the emotional capital we expend to align with just causes is not based on propaganda or hyperbole. But how can we know with certainty? How can we press forward with confidence and certitude and commitment to our cause without a thorough understanding of its underlying principles? Again, we need are in desperate need of definition.

Instead of spreading good and goodwill, under the guise of a savvy yet indefinable label (like social justice, human rights, etc.), they can use cunning and stealth while spreading death, destruction and other horrible evils. As already noted, before embarking on helping or advocating for any justice cause, the most important tool an individual must possess is an understanding about precisely what the cause is, and how well it correlates to the propitiation of humanity. This is what produces effective action. In essence, in order to zealously progress in precipitating effective actions that would help us solve the cause that holds our attention and passions, we need to get to the point of the matter by identifying the elemental crux (or heart) of our cause.

It can be confirmed that we have gotten to the crux of a cause when we can answer at least two basic questions:

1. What is the clear universal definition of the cause?
2. If solved, how does it add or enhance all of humanity?

Let's use slavery to make this point. Slavery has a universal definition, and even to this day the impact it has on all of humanity is manifest; irrespective of times (from Biblical up to our current times) or place (any geography, society or cultures), slavery is universally recognized as a scourge against all humanity. What about "social justice"? Many would proudly refer to themselves as social justice advocates, but can they confirm a universally accepted definition, and confirm its impact on humanity? Can social justice be accurately defined and correlated at all?

A quick Internet search on either Bing or Google produces seemingly countless definitions and references for the term "social justice." Predictably and seemingly fortuitously, none of the definitions are actually consistent with others. It is impossible to clarify, define and ultimately solve something that conveniently changes and morphs on a continual basis. Again, Hitler and Stalin railed against all dissenters and unified the masses while postulating they (personally) were "social justice" proponents and advocates! After careful review of various Internet sites and reference materials on social justice, we can begin to see a pattern of the rather nebulous nature of the distinction.

BusinessDictionary.com, says "Social Justice" is defined as:

> *"The fair and proper administration of laws conforming to the natural law that all persons, irrespective of ethnic origin, gender, possessions, race, religion, etc., are to be treated equally and without prejudice."*

Wikipedia defines "Social justice" as:

> *"[R]efer[ing] to the idea of creating a society or institution that is based on the principles of equality and solidarity, that understands and values human rights, and that recognizes the dignity of every human being."*

Center of Economic and Social Justice defines "Social Justice" as:

> *"[G]iving to each what he or she is due." The problem is knowing what is 'due'. Functionally, 'justice' is a set of universal principles which guide people in judging what is right and what is wrong, no matter what culture and society they live in. Justice is one of the four 'cardinal virtues' of classical moral philosophy, along with courage, temperance (self-control) and prudence (efficiency). (Faith, hope and charity are considered to be the three "religious" virtues.) Virtues or 'good habits' help individuals to develop fully their human potentials, thus enabling them to serve their own self-interests as well as work in harmony with others for their common good. The ultimate purpose of all the virtues is to elevate the dignity and sovereignty of the human person."*

With just these few examples, it is abundantly clear the definitions and underlying principles for social justice vary depending on the author. This is illuminating, but more than that, it is acute and problematic! Invariably it confirms that social justice does not meet the aforementioned criteria (concise definition and impact on humanity). Again, if a cause cannot be specifically defined and its impact confirmed, effective actions that would provide an enduring zeal and unification of the masses, cannot be achieved.

During the many workshops, speaking engagements and discussions I have participated in throughout the country, I also found a lack of clear definition. When I press the audience to work toward narrowing the words and attributes they think define social justice, the word they always arrive at is the rather vague term, "*fairness.*"

Regrettably, there is a pattern of many well-meaning, earnest and good-hearted people who have invested their emotion and passions into strict alignment with rhetoric of a movement, but not necessarily in the reality of the principles movement. If something cannot be defined, it cannot have core attributable principles. This is undeniably true! If people don't really have clear understanding of the object of their outrage (or concern), they really don't have a "just cause." At the very least, the leaders of movements should be able to properly characterize and define the movement and the respective "end game" for humanity. Social justice then, while it may have perceived understanding and following, is currently devoid of what is required for enduring practicality and unified momentum. This means, for all intents and purposes, Pastors/Priests, community leaders, and politicians (and the like) are all following a mantra fundamentally based on emotion, not on a commitment to justly justice. Again, justly justice is (by definition) definable, measureable and therefore confirmable by outcomes that are grounded in righteous and consistent foundations that promote all of humanity. What we see are coordinated movements with good intentions, but a general lack of clarity around the commitment to all humanity to benefit. This begs the question, "does this same level of ambiguity exist for 'Racial Justice' and 'Human Rights' as well?"

When searching for definitions for the term "Racial justice", we find there are very few actual definitions. Of the definitions and references found, there are no quantitative definitions. Most definitions are presented as fairly broad social statements. For instance, according to the Hyams Foundation:

> *"Racial justice is a proactive reinforcement of policies, practices, attitudes and actions that produce equitable power, access, opportunities, treatment, impacts and outcomes for all."*

Again, the lack of specifically defined and very clear quantifiable distinctions open the door for potential misuse of the public goodwill that would express passion and support for the cause. Having no concise definition is again problematic. How are people expected to rally around a cause that can't be quantified and clearly defined? How can a movement that seeks to propel people into action legitimately exist without a discernable objective and specific criteria for confirming success? Looking back at base criteria, "racial justice" (in its current state) cannot be construed as a just cause. At some point we should ask if it makes sense to want to invest time, energies, and emotional capital in something that (based on research) seems wholly contrived (for mostly "political" ends) instead representing attributes of what would be deemed a just cause.

The term "Human Rights" has seemingly been a term used since the beginning of time. Of all fervent causes, human rights seems to innately capture our hearts and imaginations of what we would perceive as injustices. Since we would assume base recognition of natural law (recognizing God, nature and morality), human rights should be readily identifiable and defined; it should be logically self-evident! Since the term is self-illuminating (i.e., "human" referring to what it means to be human, and "rights" referring to basic rights of man) we should expect consistent, clear and concise definitions. Ironically, this is not necessarily the case.

According to the Bing dictionary definition, human rights are defined as:

> *"Freedom, justice, and equality: the rights that are considered by most societies to belong automatically to everyone, e.g. the rights to freedom, justice, and equality"*

The Merriam Webster dictionary defines human rights as:

> *"Regarded as belonging fundamentally to all persons". The basic rights and freedoms to which all humans are entitled, often held to include the right to life*

and liberty, freedom of thought and expression, and equality before the law."

Wikipedia describes human rights as:
Moral principles that set out certain standards of human behavior, and are regularly protected as legal rights in national and international law. They are "commonly understood as inalienable fundamental rights to which a person is inherently entitled simply because she or he is a human being." Human rights are thus conceived as universal (applicable everywhere) and egalitarian (the same for everyone).

There are countless other human rights definitions, but these three examples were used just to further the discussion and illuminate our plight. "Human Rights" is not concisely defined, nor does it have specific criteria (measureable) that would confirm whether we are making incremental progress or have achieved success. If we consider U.S. laws (including the Declaration of Independence and U.S. Constitution), there are already many laws that protect against the aforementioned definitions of human rights violations; human rights, as has been broadly defined, is unlawful as prescribed by U.S. law. But the fact is, there are many within the U.S. and throughout the world that would argue the U.S. violates human rights. How and why does this disconnect occur?

Even within the governing bodies of the United Nations, human rights violations are condemned and rejected, yet some countries who participate in what could be argued as various forms of human rights violations, are respected members of the U.N. The point is, irrespective as to whether a term has been used since the beginning of man and is fully "mature" (as with human rights), or is relatively new (as with social justice and racial justice), we are still faced with an overwhelming void in the lack of clarity about what these terms actually mean. Further, because of the lack clarity, it is not clear when injustices actually occur, or how/when we will know whether progress is being made (even if incremental) to cure it.

We are left with still trying to figure out how are we to best advocate for what we believe are "just causes" when we don't even know the definition and criteria that undergird them? How are we to produce effective actions, and commit ourselves to help solve the most pressing social concerns and issues of our times, when they are ill-defined? Why do all of these social/cultural issues appear to be purposely vague? Why, after all this time, have these oft-spoken injustices been left relatively obscured?

There are many like myself who are wholly vested in movements and causes strictly because they are sensitive to the plight of the most innocent. But, also, I have come to find there are equally as many who are strictly committed to these issues for notoriety and personal gain. History is replete with examples that confirm strategic reasons for creating obscure distinctions and starting movements; powerful people and worldwide organizations advance and emerge from them! Political leaders and leaders of movements (whether or not motivated with nefarious intent) find there is unlimited power that can be garnered, harvested and consolidated unto themselves if they can unscrupulously play on emotions of people who trust in a common theme of "injustice." This is a well-known fact and regrettably has been successfully repeated throughout history. The sad fact is, instead of operating from clear altruistic motives that unite people and help move humanity forward, those who are insidiously unprincipled create distinctions and use ill-defined social/cultural movements for personal aggrandizement or to gain politically by feigning sympathy. While it may sound quite wholly manipulative and scripted, the ability to generate emotions like outrage and disgust can provide people, political parties, or organizations with the ability to masquerade under the (previously noted) ill-defined banner of social justice, racial justice or human rights; this provides career acceleration and the ability to generate and maximize donations, while also giving "license" to operate with obscurity and with no accountability for actual results.

As a matter of basic human behavior, if an object that prompts disgust and outrage can be made to become an isolated target and focus of our attention, a strategic mis-direction occurs which would allow perpetuation of nefarious acts without personal accountability. Again, Hitler, Stalin, Lenin, Mao, Mussolini, and Castro were all masters at this; we now see that their collective notorious deeds are responsible for the worst human scourge in the history of mankind, rendering over 100 million deaths while their respective populations festered in a relative stupor.

Please know, while we have taken a critical look at trying to discern exactly what constitutes a "just cause" (especially as it relates to social justice, racial justice and human rights), the intent is not to begrudge or condemn, rather to just sound a caution. The caution is simply to arm us with facts so we don't unwittingly invest our time, emotional energies, sweat-equity, and lofty donations in causes still yet to be defined. Before investing anything, we should uncover the fundamental underlying principles that undergird the cause. Principles are the principal thing! If primacy is given to principles, we can adopt core principles and gain footing with any of these respective causes and begin to aggressively move forward with them as exemplary justly just causes.

In summary of this chapter, we found there is an unacceptable and inexcusable lack of proper definitions and context for social justice, racial justice and human rights. While these distinctions have been around for over a hundred years, they still lack clarity. As purely emotional issues, they have actually successfully manufactured a base consisting of masses of people around the globe. If they are to be really effective in actually combating and solving problems however, concise definitions and clarity about measureable outcome(s) are dutifully required. Even with the relative lack of definable objectivity, all is not lost, as essentially the only thing required (at this point) is objective clarity about what is real/true justice at the core; identification of core 1st principles. Then, and only then, will these movements be able to appropriately reframe and refocus in order to operate in a holistically coherent way for moving forward. This requires the identification and adherence to principles.

Finding underlying principles seems like a logical and prudent exercise, but we now know how easily masses of people can be manipulated with clever marketing, populist messaging, charismatic personalities, and vague distinctions. So, how can we earnestly thwart attempts to misuse and abuse our good intentions going forward? Most importantly, how are we to guard ourselves from people (or organizations) that may have questionable character and nefarious contemptible intent, from misinforming and manipulating us into wholly supporting their cause? The answer is easy; it boils down to 1st principles!

Chapter Three

PRINCIPLES OR PRINCIPALITES

For whom will we serve?

"In any compromise between good and evil, it is only evil that can profit."

~Ayn Rand

This book is not a referendum on the various justice causes or agencies. It is strictly intended to help prevent misuse and abuse of the well-meaning. By instilling practices that help focus on making sure allegiances are based on definable and measurable causes, the unscrupulous are prevented from garnering support for a movement by simply twisting and manipulating language and distinctions designed to take advantage of human sensibilities. The goal is to prevent further abuses that tend to do nothing more than help the unprincipled garner power, while becoming permanently ensconced in some form of political/leadership. Before going further, we are at a point when we must ask ourselves, "based on accurate history of how 'justice' (in general) have been used for nefarious 'political' ends, are we primarily committed to the various justice causes for political means (i.e. to align with mantras of political/party id, personal gain, etc.)? Or, are we defiantly committed to, as a matter of 1st principle, helping ensure the standard 'justly justice' is proliferated across all humanity?

What we can confirm at this point is, when it's all said and done, the sincere and well-meaning are just desiring to help show compassion to those who are put upon by others; they are committed to simply helping the least among us - the "poor"!

If we review the various definitions for social justice, racial justice and human rights, while they are all different, they do present some common core threads. If we were to truncate and crystalize the common threads, we would arrive at some basic principles all these distinctions have in common. One basic tenet underlying and unifying these causes is the principle of "fairness." Basic fairness is often the single clarifying characteristic that is used to summarize injustices.

When I speak to large audiences and attempt to narrow the meaning of social justice, fairness is universally accepted the principal issue. When racial justice is narrowed, again fairness is the issue. And, when human rights is focused and narrowed, it boils down to the extension of fairness towards all humankind. Fairness is a consistently held unifying principle with seemingly all movements portending to end injustice!

If we are honest with ourselves, we have now entered into another relative conundrum, because how can we define fairness? Is it simply that everyone has the exact same provisions and outcomes as everyone else? If so, in the pursuit of fairness, would it mean that unless all humankind exists under conditions that are strictly egalitarian, there is fundamental injustice? If that's the case, are we supposed to defer and consolidate powers unto governments/leaders to be the arbiter of justice? In context, the rise of the most evil persons in history were due to the fact they sounded the alarm of "injustice," carried the banner of "fairness" and demanded consolidation of powers to themselves. This resulted in the worst death, destruction and mayhem with over 100 million deaths. Is strict egalitarianism possible at all? If we stick with fairness alone as our principle, all these are factors must be considered, and all questions must be answered. The fact is, the pursuit of fairness alone would be impossible and notably disastrous!

"Fairness," when defined as some form of equality (of existence, experiences and outcomes),is an impossibility. The cacophony of huge variances that instinctively propel human action, bolstered by our innate dynamic nature, makes this notion downright silly. If we fervently believe in fairness as previously defined, we should consider and question, "is God fair?" Wisely, we could conclude no! God is not "fair" (as defined by egalitarian means), He is wholly Holy and "just"! God did not design or intend that humankind should be robots existing with the same base structures and producing the exact same rote and predictable ends. He put varying skills, talents and abilities in each of us, virtually ensuring differing outcomes. In God's eyes, it is an anathema for man to supplant His divine and vibrant nature and replace it with an egalitarian mindset bent toward egalitarian ends. Fundamentally, this is not fairness at all; this is the embodiment of distorted obedience to structural enslavement that can lead to manifest evils (already noted). Man cannot be free and express his fullness of liberty while being wholly committed to egalitarianism. With that said, liberty and freedom are mutually exclusive with the definition of "fairness" (with the goal of egalitarianism). While fairness as it relates to equal outcomes is a flawed definition and pursuit, a better definition that would connote a modicum of fairness while presenting a richer and more measurable definition, is "justly justice." Again, rightly defined, justly justice is a righteous, true and irreproachable principle of justice impartially extended to ***all*** mankind. If fairness is replaced with justly justice and narrowly defined as encouraging and honoring the essence of all "human existence," we can indeed confirm God is "just,"and progress our argument for supporting justice (as it relates to just being able to "exist" alongside others) as a core principle for ending manifest injustices.

With a commitment to an uncompromising standard of justly justice, this primary principle will drive all of our donations, support, and encouragement of people and/or agencies for justice. Our tendencies and traditions will be replaced with a renewed standard of justice that is definable, consistent and fully coherent with principles that extend the same base level of good to all of humanity. It will fundamentally override our normal triggers and emotions, and compel us to act with only the purest heart-felt motives as we take a stand, march/protest and go to the ballot box! What we will see is, justly justice creates it own perpetual motion, momentum and longevity based on a consistent stand to eliminate all injustice in the best interest for all humanity.

The biggest problem with manifold labels of injustice is, while it can't be readily defined, we do know it when we see it. Slavery was a clearly manifest gross injustice. The holocaust was a human scourge and grave injustice. The underlying problem with both these historically significant and notable events was there was a complete rejection of human existence. Both instances characterized some people as mere objects (or somehow subhuman), while celebrating life and existence of others. Governments during these periods, specifically objectified certain groups of humans as being somehow subhuman, and made them objects of collective scorn. There was no commitment to honoring and respecting all humans as merely having the right to exist. If people would have (at the very least) had a base commitment to just tolerate and recognize the inherent right for other people to simply exist, these atrocities would not have occurred. The grim reality is, there was no baseline of toleration, and certainly no extension of grace, honor and respect for certain members of humankind to simply exist. "Existence" must be a core principle of justice.

To exact an effective working definition and provide clarity for what constitutes injustice, a transition of thought and terminology must take place; the demand of equal outcomes, must be replaced to a new focus on an equal baseline of respect for human existence. Honoring human existence is the core of justice! This means the commitment to allowing **all** humankind to emerge, so we can appropriately come along side and encourage its growth, is fundamental. With that said, lets confirm and define then that "the collective commitment to come alongside of **all** humanity and encourage its development," must be the unifying principle for **all** justice movements! This definition fully encapsulates the essence of all the aforementioned definitions of social justice, racial justice and human rights, and should therefore represent all these movements as the core principle.

The core principle of a commitment to "existence" seems easy, but in reality how does this simple distinction translate within the missions and outcomes of existing movements? Key terms from the various definitions of social justice appear to reflect a commitment to mere human existence. Terms like *"fairness," "equal treatment," "giving each what he or she is due,"* and *"dignity and sovereignty of every human being"* are pronounced as actionable for social justice. Racial justice also seems to commit to the support of mere existence; it uses terms like *equitable power, access, opportunities, treatment, impacts and outcomes for all*. Human Rights culminates with a commitment to all human existence with terms like, "*freedom, justice and equality belonging fundamentally to all persons,*" "*basic* rights and *freedoms to which all humans are entitled,*" "*inalienable fundamental rights to which a person is inherently entitled simply because she or he is a human being.*" There is a single common denominator that calls for respecting a base level of human existence in all these definitions, and this is notably the central unifying point!

There is now no doubt about the fact that *existence* is the key and unassailable root to solving injustice. The question we should ask is, Why do so many of these movements still have inconsistent and incoherent policies that seem to conflict with the very nature and intent of what they purport? If fairness and inalienable rights boil down to a core principle of the right to simply exist (for all humankind), why have social justice, racial justice and human rights proponents (organizations and individuals) adopted (perhaps unwittingly) the same path of racist slave owners and genocidal dictators that came before them? Remember, genocidal dictatorial regimes of the past simply played with language, cleverly renaming and reframing/re-classifying what is "human," The truth is, while these agencies (many well-meaning) rail about injustice by giving all humankind inalienable fundamental rights, they also rather duplicitously stand with/for denying the extension of the right to "exist" to the most innocent among us! I recognize this may be an inconvenient truth that's hard to fathom. It's difficult to wrap our hearts and minds around an indictment that says the very people and agencies who are purportedly committed to ending injustice, actually have no aptitude for following through on their base commitment; but for the most part, they are in many ways actually complicit with injustice by denying the extension of the inalienable right for all humankind to merely exist.

As a businessman and as president of the Frederick Douglass Foundation of California, I have been blessed to be able to travel across the world. During many of my travels, I am asked to speak about basic issues of life and their historical connection of the issues faced during the life and times of the honorable Frederick Douglass. During most of my speaking engagements and workshops, questions about social justice, racial justice and human rights are frequently asked. Instead of launching headlong into what can be characterized as systemic concealment by the various organization/agencies (and people) who advocate for "justice," I ask participants to participate in a simple exercise so they can arrive at their own definitions and conclusions. The exercise simply asks participants to envision a caricature (in their own minds) of the worst, most offensive, poorest, most needy, most put-upon, most maligned among us. After they have it pictured in their minds, I then ask them to give details. Invariably, most people provide caricatures of homeless men (sometimes women), who haven't bathed, have no money, no family, and no hope. I prod them deeper. I ask, "Would he be worse off if he were stuck in this condition before he's a grown man (i.e., if he were a child)?" The answer is invariably yes! Followed up by the fact that a child is even more defenseless with no means, no family, no possibility for working (earning income), and no representation for justice. Going deeper, I ask "Would the child be even worse off if he were a toddler and couldn't walk or talk?" Then, "What about if he were still in the womb?" At this point, participants eyes open wide; some participants express true contrition at the realization that while they have steadfastly and zealously stood for helping "the poor," they have somehow been veiled from seeing the poorest, most needy, most innocent, and defenseless among us are those in the womb. Invariably, it becomes clear that the most innocent among us, having absolutely no "voice" (literally or figuratively), and with no possibility of securing their own future or making their own way, are the pre-born.

By virtue of definitions, historical context, and our current social construct, it is undeniable that "justice" begins in the womb! God, by His divine providence sees and defines it that way, and if we are completely honest with ourselves, it is the only irreproachable fundamental base determinant that provides a consistent definition and basis of measurement for all "justice" causes. With that said, this is the definition of Justly Justice! Real, Justly Justice is defined as the equal right to life for all mankind through support and encouragement of the base level of *existence.* After reviewing all definitions for the various causes, it would be wholly inconsistent and hypocritical for any agencies (purportedly standing for justice) to dismiss the fundamental right to exist as a precondition and essential tenet that drives their actions and activities. What should be asked is, Do all social justice, racial justice and human rights organizations affirm the right to existence (a fundamental right to life) as elemental to their cause? As a matter of 1st principles, do they insist on a commitment to "existence" as a primary goal and focal point that helps characterize, define and measure their overall effectiveness?

This chapter is entitled "principles or principalities." It should now be more evident as to why this was the chosen title and what this means. Essentially, it confirms that in the end, we can't have it both ways! Either we will ardently, fervently and principally stand on foundational principles that bring clarity and consistently to our hearts desire for helping ensure "justice" for all humankind (by standing for life/existence for all), or we will double-down and serve principalities (leaders and "masterminds" with diabolical motives and mindsets) who have cleverly veiled and concealed underlying inconsistencies in order to use and manipulate movements for political or selfish ends! This is the "aha-moment" that demands a response. Whom will we serve? Are we primarily politically motivated, and will therefore defend or eschew the connecting of dots, and historical facts already confirmed? Or, will we embrace "the veil" being lifted, our hearts celebrating (in now knowing the truth), and with new rigor and anticipation look to proceed?

In summary of this chapter, we have now come to the heart of the matter of justly justice. We now see and appreciate that irrespective of the causes we may have been involved with, by their own definition there is purportedly a core principle of justice they all share; this invariably means honoring existence for all. The heart of this matter is, we have new understanding and better illumination into what truly constitutes justice; now, we can appropriately discern the truth. With that in mind, justly justice demands an answer! For whom will we choose to serve, "principals or principalities" indeed.

Chapter Four

THE HEART OF THE MATTER IS THE HEART!

"There is no safety for honest men except by believing all possible evil of evil men."

~Edmund Burke

What has been dealt with thus far is the result of methodically lifting a veritable veil so we can see what's behind and under the "curtain" of justice. We have been able to uncover that there are many seemingly well-intended justice movements, that are somehow nebulous and ill-defined, which has allowed the most evil genocidal dictators throughout history to use to their benefit while propagating unmentionable death and destruction. By focusing on finding a central and fundamental principle, we have also been able to better define (using their own respective definitions) the actual and true definition of justice movements. This exercise helped confirm the heart of all justice movements is not the subjective distinctions of "fairness," rather it is the support and encouragement of "existence" -all human existence. This is the crux of the matter, and 1st principle, for what true justice movements must embrace if they are to be consistent with their respective charter and thwart cries of hypocrisy.

To begin solving and combatting issues of injustice, we have to look at the heart. There are two aspects of the heart that must be dealt with; one is public, and one personal. The public aspect revolves around just getting to the "heart" of the matter of properly and succinctly defining justice; in this case, we focused attention on taking out obscurities in order to define, crystallize and narrow down "justice" to its most basic element and central issue. The other side of the heart is the personal side. In this case, we introspectively look at our own heart to confirm what's truly in it (i.e., to confirm our own true motivations and actual commitment to justice).

The heart represents the core of who we are; it is what defines our being, as it is the central and innermost part of our being from which all issues flow. With the heart we feel love, we sympathize, and we are motivated and prompted with zeal to act (among countless other things); it should be noted, all things related to righteousness and justice emanate from the heart. Likewise, evil can also fester and manifest itself in the heart. The Bible confirms, "out of the abundance of the heart, the mouth speaks." Ultimately, it is the heart that drives all our actions while it also characterizes who we are at our core. Lying, duplicitousness and any penchant toward insincerity all play a part in our personal integrity, and can be fully exposed by just looking at the heart. With that said, if we want to be effective, we cannot truly commit ourselves to involvement in arenas that combat the issues of injustice until we can appropriately confirm and resolve what's truly in our own hearts.

After delving into the heart of the matter as it pertains to justice and confirming that the central basic principle of justice is simply respecting existence, our actions going forward will indicate whether we truly have a heart for our respective cause. Actions and intent to support causes that herald "justice," "equal rights," or "equality," without those causes being wholly committed to the fundamental commitment to life/existence, would be hypocritical; it would show our heart is misaligned with our purported commitment.

At this point, we should ask ourselves, Do I have a heart of malice and one that is calloused, consistent with the hearts of others who denied the basic right to "existence" (like the slave owners and dictators) of the past? Or, Is my heart sensitive, loving and compassionate to the extent it is wholly committed to ensure justice by strictly reflecting that all my actions and allegiances align with the core principle of life? What is your real heart? Is it truly motivated by righteousness and justice for the poor and the most innocent among us? Is it primarily concerned with political party or movements, and the basic issue of life/existence is secondary? Does your heart stand firm in truth, or is it willing to believe in anything as long as it aligns with personal (self-centered) gain? These are important questions to consider as they will help discover your true heart and who you are at the core of your being.

The goal of this book, and necessary introspection, is again not a rebuke or reprimand. It is intended to provide clarity for justice causes (and our support thereof) so we can more strongly identify, unify and become truly effective. We can no longer allow usurpers to "hijack" well-meaning altruistic movements that honor basic existence. Too many times in history, slick politicians have easily sailed into office by simply stating, "I am a proponent of social justice." Too many churches and denominations have been duped into voting for people, even though they have been wholly antithetical and antagonistic to their cause (Bible), simply because they (or their respective political party) spout the terms social justice, racial justice, human rights, and equality. Too many people have lost their lives and freedoms due to unscrupulous people hell-bent (literally) on deceiving and misdirecting, while perpetrating evil machinations. Too many have been duped into giving their hard-earned monies, sweat equity and life commitment to special interests/movements, simply because they rant and rail for "justice", but at the same time, they support the worst and most heinous injustices. These are all matters of the heart!

If the heart is wicked, wickedness will manifest. If the heart is committed to love, love will prevail! Love is the perfect neutralizer and sanitizer for the heart. Love, in its simplest form, is just commitment to the *existence* and to the *service* to another. When we hear that we should love one another, at a base level, this what is required. If we reflect back on the caricature I posited about what would be an example of the worst off among us, we initially confirmed that the homeless man on the street, who hadn't bathed, etc., would be the worst. The fundamental reason why that poor person, while enduring the most regrettable of circumstances, is not the worst of the worst off, is because he lives! Because he has existence, he has received love (via birth, at the very least); because he was graciously granted the gift of life, he now possesses the possibility of living life to the fullest. Even a homeless child wandering around in the worst living conditions on the planet (albeit enduring incredible hardship) at least has the possibility of improving his condition. So again, the worst of the worst off are those having no voice, no possibility to survive on their own, and whose possibility of just existing is completely at the mercy of someone else; these are undeniably the unborn. Regrettably, they are the most innocent and put-upon, while also being the most maligned single demographic in the history of mankind. So how did we get here? A purposeful look at history will definitively confirm a battle that has raged since the beginning of man to eradicate the unborn. It is important to understand why we have this battle, and confirm why and how we arrived at a point in our history whereby we brazenly endorse and celebrate the single most evil injustice man has ever known.

In summary, this chapter confirms the heart is desperate! It is either desperately wicked, or desperately good. It is also the core and pinnacle of who we are at the core of our being. This leaves us with the ability to confirm whether we are who we think we are (that being, good, honest and sincerely looking to extend the best of goodness to all mankind), or deceived, duplicitous, contrived, and wicked! Again, we can't have it both ways. Irrespective of the stories we tell ourselves, the actions we produce will support one and reject the other, and that will confirm who we are at heart.

Chapter Five

WHOLLY HOLY?

Can wholly incoherent and Holy inconsistent offer "justice"?

"Men never do evil so completely and cheerfully as when they do it from religious conviction."

~Blaise Pascal

What has been uncovered thus far is a working definition of what quantifies justly justice, and our role and commitment to exalt it as a 1st core principle. These new concepts alone should have all principled people perceiving this book as a harbinger of good news and glad tidings! It should help mitigate any further wasted time or resources on any movements (including people and politicians) other than those upholding the standards of celebrating the right to exist for all humankind.

Due to "heart strings" tied to political/party's, traditions, ideology, idolatry and the commitment to support individuals irrespective to what they stand for, there is no delusion that some people will remain stubbornly entrenched and unmoved about what has been uncovered; many are already trying to conjure up a "back-door" way out, as they play mental gymnastics in an attempt to figure out ways to affirm what can only be described (at this point) as manifestly incoherent and irrational.

Fortunately, because of the basic tenets of the justice movements, human history, and God's Word, there is no way out of this relative conundrum. To the prudent and principled, transition to this simple concept of justice is "easy" and matter-of-fact. We either stand for the right to exist as a matter of 1st principle, or we stand with the many nefarious genocidal maniacs of the past! I realize this pat answer is still too coy for some, but the good news is, we haven't even begun to scratch the surface of this issue; there is an incredible amount to additional "due-diligence" yet to uncover. Regardless of how you feel at the moment, I have no doubt we will achieve an uncompromising and unified commitment to 1st principles after we delve into a more thorough understanding of history. In the end, we will have the full capacity reject all that is wholly incoherent while becoming "Holy" consistent with our move toward justly justice.

We should now recognize that in order to assert justice of any sort as a simple baseline tenet, agencies (including individuals and/or political entities) must support the notion that justice begins with the mere extension of allowing one to exist. This is not "rocket science"; it should now be quite obvious and promoted as a matter of fact. Any who do not wholly support this notion as a matter of a 1st foundational principle cannot honestly assert they are justice-minded and-focused. They may be well-intended, but at best, they are hypocritically living as a contradiction to themselves. With these types of individuals, political motivations, money motivations or some other agendas are likely overriding logic, prudence, and commitment to humanity. Our attempt is to hone in on and ferret out *all* agendas that are wholly incoherent with the justice movement so we can appropriately intervene with the very institutions we have invested our heart and passions for justice; we want to prevent misuse by people and organizations that inexplicably and incoherently reject the basic need of existence for the poorest and most innocent among us. Again, the accurate understanding of history provides answers as to the foundations and basis that encourages the rise of institutions and movements operating in wholly incoherent while being "Holy" inconsistent against the perpetuation of humanity.

Starting with the beginning of man, history definitively and unequivocally connect-the-dots confirming how entire societies arrive at a point that it casually disregards the poorest and most needy segments of humanity. Individually, through intense introspection, we must exercise rigor in order to reconcile how we are somehow able to supplant and placate our conscience while supporting affronts against humanity, and cavalierly lauding and applauding ourselves while doing it! A simple example of this is, many will stand for and endorse agencies and political candidates who purport social justice, while they (at the same time) support denying or restricting life for the poorest and most needy (as previously defined). How? Why? This is clearly hypocritical and incoherent! Something is very wrong when we can't see the grotesque hypocrisy of ranting and protesting in outrage (under the banner of whatever our "justice "cause), while concurrently allowing the cause to remain quiet and complicit when it comes to assuring the most basic principle of human existence (life) is extended to all humankind. If we are wholly committed to spreading justice across all humanity, why haven't we been able to discern (at least to this point) this absurd hypocrisy?

The fact is, our eyes have been veiled and obscured by lofty new mantras and distinctions, charismatic personalities, and by uniquely disguised (yet manifestly evil) strategies specifically hatched to eliminate targeted segments of the poor/needy. There is no doubt, general lack of the capacity to observe historical knowledge and context has blinded and deceived us, but history provides the remedy for lifting the veil! Accurate characterization, interpretation and context of history will now be our focus!

From the beginning of mankind a battle was initiated, and that battle still rages today; the battle has always been between "good" and "evil." In Genesis 3:15, God drew permanent, perpetual battle lines between good and evil. The crux of the verse can be summarized, "…I (God) will put enmity between you (evil one) and the woman ...and her offspring…" (Gen 3:15). From that moment, evil was put on notice and proceeded to exact revenge on all of God's creation. Most importantly, the focus of evil's revenge, plans and tactics to consistently act against and undermine God and His creation involved targeting "the woman and her offspring." Evil was motivated by one primary goal, and that goal was to restrict or prevent "life." Current populist themes connote there is a "war on women"; it is affirmative that evil definitely persists with this. But in relation and context to humanity, our current characterization and interpretation of this "war" is "Holy" inconsistent and inaccurate! From the beginning of time, women have been part of a battle, but it revolves around God battling evil in a war *for* women…and her offspring!

The Bible makes clear that God alone is the giver of life. Numerous Psalms and verses confirm this, but Psalm 139 is especially telling. In Psalms 139 13-15, king David proclaims, "For You did form my inward parts; You did knit me together in my mother's womb. will confess *and* praise You *for You are fearful and wonderful and* for the awful wonder of my birth! Wonderful are Your works, and that my inner self knows right well. My frame was not hidden from You when I was being formed in secret [and] intricately *and* curiously wrought in the depths of the earth." There are many verses confirming God's intricate handiwork as He specifically zealously initiates humankind from conception, as a never-ending testament to His divine authority and greatness. In Jeremiah, the prophet reminds of God's greatness and confirms God's specific designs for each life. Jeremiah 1:5 reads, "Before I formed you in the womb I knew [and] approved of you, and before you were born I separated *and* set you apart, consecrating you." It is incontrovertible that God intricately ordains and designs each individual from conception, and has manifold plans for each life to come forth. The fact is, the perpetuation of humankind brings glory to God, and acts as a constant reminder of His sovereignty and might as He fights specifically for women (universally) and her offspring. In the most horrific ways, evil has sought to pervert, undermine and prevent the awesome plan for life by specifically strategically attacking the most innocent in this battle, the baby.

The Bible is replete with assaults on the baby (born and unborn). There have been many pharaohs, kings, and idols/idol gods that have channeled evil and demanded the killing of children. The most memorable of these demented proclamations (to kill all children) is during the times of Moses' birth, and during the birth of Jesus. But throughout history, the fervent commitment to idol gods and idol worship has claimed countless innocents. Regrettably, even to this day, the commitment to "idols" (whether persons/personalities, political affiliation's, movements, etc.) continues to wreak havoc on God's divine plan for His creation.

Only the most radical and quite extreme mindsets would solicit and empower ideology that prevents mere existence from coming forth. Some of these mindsets and ideologies have horribly manifested and are indelibly part of U.S. history. What if we were to intently look at what could only be construed as representative examples of horrid atrocities fundamentally enshrined in U.S. history? Could we "stomach" such a look? Would we quickly dismiss and reject facts and history to preserve our own ties and "heart strings"? Would we excuse and deny? Well, let's see! Let's take a step-by-step, precept-on-precept, look at two of the most controversial issues of our time: racism and abortion! Ironically, while these two different paradigms are seemingly disconnected, are actually very closely tied. Because they are so closely tied, let's look at them both concurrently!

As we know, during the 1800s, African-American slavery was still allowed and "respected." Rape among the slave women was running rampant during this dreadful time in American history. The quintessential women's rights pioneer, Susan B. Anthony, rose to prominence as a result of helping with all aspects of "women's suffrage." The Honorable Susan B. Anthony was not a respecter of persons; her tireless works helped ease the horrible suffering for all women, including prostitutes and slaves. As you can imagine, slave women endured the worst of suffering; many endured horrific rapes, and then were forced to put their bodies through primitive and barbaric forms of abortion. Often, the "masters" used and heralded the evils of abortion to salve for their debased conscience. They conveniently hid acts of indignity and indiscretions precipitated on slaves by forcing many of them to abort their children.

Wholly incoherent and manifestly debased mindsets believed forced abortions performed on slaves and prostitutes were actually humanitarian acts, and somehow demonstrated acts of "compassion." Their deluded mindset was that no slave (or prostitute) could ever want their children to exist, while being born into (and relegated to) dreadful and meager conditions; they held the opinion that being born a slave was worse than being born at all. Therefore, abortion was heralded as the "compassionate cure" for many pregnant slave women. How is this at all conceivable? How can it be that abortion was actually humanitarian and compassionate for those who lived during these dreadful times of extreme hardship? Regrettably, this mindset still exists today; since it is a remedy that purportedly helps absolve perpetual hardship and poverty, in some elitist circles abortion is *really* viewed as an act of compassion toward "the poor"! Gaining accurate perspective from an actual slave provides valuable insight into these questions and complexities.

Frederick Douglass was not only our first civil rights pioneer, but he also pioneered advocacy for women's rights and human rights; he worked tirelessly, and was simpatico with both Susan B. Anthony and Harriet Tubman. While working with Ms. Anthony, Mr. Douglass was quite opinionated about abortion. While he indeed had to endure what could be argued as the worst treatment and degradation in all American history, he appropriately considered abortion as an evisceration of the core principles that connect and uphold humanity. This is telling! To put it into proper perspective, Frederick Douglass was born as a product of his mother being raped (by a slave master), he was born into a life of slavery, endured countless trials, hardship and pain (countless whippings, and having being beaten to within an inch of death), and still had the principled foresight to know that even he had it far better as compared to the poorest and most needy…the unborn!

Frederick Douglass' commitment to justice for all humanity, overrode the contorted illogical practicalities of the idea abortion as being some kind arcane form of compassion and humanitarianism. As regrettable as the horrific circumstances he had to endure, he was delighted to have been given the right to exist so he can have the possibility of living life to the fullest; if the pre-born are precluded from the right to exist, they have no such possibility, and by definition, this is the absolute poorest and most needy segment of all humanity. Mr. Douglass' life proves the point about what's possible once life is granted. He went from living a quite meager existence and escaped from the various vestiges of the worst of abject slavery into a life of unparalleled victory!

In spite of what Frederick Douglass endured, he principally fought for justice (the right to just merely exist). After recognizing his plight (born as a slave, hated and abused) along with his ardent stand as a statesman, all should be fully satisfied with his contention that justice indeed begins in the womb! Further, when Susan B. Anthony asked about whether there are any *exceptions* (e.g, with rape or incest), Douglass appropriately reminded and confirmed that if such exceptions were made, he quite simply wouldn't exist (notably, many of those with him wouldn't have existed either, as untold numbers of slaves were born as a result of rape and incest)!

What is greatly needed today are people of 1st principles like Douglass. History confirms that Frederick Douglass stood for what was right even when it was inconvenient; he actually went against his esteemed political/party. When Douglass realized the truth about his allegiance to a political party that was the party of slavery (and abortion), he swore off the party! He found the Party was not committed to ensuring life liberty and the pursuit of happiness for all mankind, so he matter-of-factly concluded it did not deserve his allegiance. Can we do this? If we find our beloved political party is not committed to the 1st principle of justice (life), how many are principled enough to take such an uncompromising stand in these days and times? It seems to me political parties, politicians and "special interests" are verifiable stumbling blocks and strongholds for many of us today. Our goal is to somehow break the "chains" and strongholds so we can (without hypocrisy or contradiction) fully represent what we dutifully are committed to represent.

After an opportune meeting with President Abraham Lincoln, Douglass was admonished by Lincoln to read the Declaration of Independence and the U.S. Constitution. It was after reading these documents, that he found underlying principles of these precious documents that actually enhance liberty and freedom (most notably, they both also wholly support and respect "life" as a 1st principle), and he quickly became an ardent and strict Constitutionalist. He remained undyingly committed to the Constitution until his death! Again, a question worth pondering is, Are there any people committed to 1st principles today who will (after understanding life as the 1st principle of justice) stand against their preferred party and preconceived ideology? After reading this book and researching, will people still hold on to their respective party as the first, last and ONLY principle, or will they commit to "real" social justice/racial justice/human rights that has been confirmed to begin with "life"? If we are to prevail against agencies and ideologies of injustice, we must begin taking a stand for righteousness and truth instead of standing with and for manifest evil. Again, evil is targeted against all humanity, with its primary target as *"the woman and her offspring."* To fight and win in the battle we must stand *for* exalting the innate nature of God's design *for* woman and children!

Even after the scourge of slavery ended, the worst of gross injustices (due to diabolical deeds against humanity) persisted. During the 1900s, people still attempted to appease their conscience by the belief that preventing and restricting life was compassionate. The eugenics movement heralded and enshrined "selective breeding" (attempt to manipulate process of human "improvement" by eliminating "undesirables") and was actually built on this arcane insidious mindset. While it has morphed and changed over the past 60 years, eugenics is the principle that precipitated the killing of over six million Jews, and is still the underlying core principle of the current abortion movement. Most importantly, this insidious movement is the principal "engine" that precipitates the "war on women," but instead of being accurately distinguished as such, it is consistently heralded as "rights for women." This is the permanently enshrined epitome of the wholly incoherent and "Holy" inconsistent!

This chapter has confirmed that from the beginning of time a battle between good and evil rages. The battle targets all of humanity as an affront to God's creation, but because of their place in God's eyes, it is especially egregious toward *the woman and her offspring (baby)*. While Susan B. Anthony and Frederick Douglass fought to secure women's rights and thwart the evils of abortion, the underlying evil that motivates elimination of the unborn is proving insatiable. Eugenics, the social movement claiming to improve the genetic features of human populations through selective breeding, has emerged as justification for the worst human scourge ever known to man; to this day, it is still exalted by academics and elites as "enlightened" and somehow "compassionate," while it wrecks havoc on *the woman and her offspring*. The woman and her offspring *is* the battle! By just being born, we are all automatically enlisted into the battle, but we must confirm which side of the battle we're on. Are we fighting with and for God or are we on the side of evil? As with most types of evil schemes, this one has evolved and progressed to this point in our history because of the relative tolerance for the incoherent, and an overall lack of understanding and sensitivity as to what is truly consistent with "the Holy." I am hopeful the perceptible call in our own souls at this point is to *go deeper*; we can only recover our sensibilities and practicalities in these matters if we indeed go deeper in the understanding of evil as it is wholly manifested in diabolical deeds proliferated via eugenics.

Chapter Six

"YOU-GIN-IT" EUGENICS

The euphoric rise of the most evil injustice

"The hottest place in Hell is reserved for those who remain neutral in times of great moral conflict."
~ Dr. Martin Luther King Jr.

Under to guise of liberality and women's rights, the evil scourge of eugenics has been ginned and esteemed to the point it has been accepted into the psyche of the American mainstream! While it literally represents the most diabolical forms of the most grotesque debasement of humankind, it is consistently ginned (by academics, pseudo-intellectuals and elitists) as a greater good for the enlightened.

Of all evils, the worst kinds are those that are euphorically embraced and universally celebrated, while mercilessly maiming and killing innocents. It should be noted, evil has somehow been able to penetrate the human psyche to the degree it now accepts the absolute worst of all human suffering being precipitated under the guise of compassion and justice; eugenics is the primary perpetrator, and has always been dutifully packaged as a form of compassion. Because it is esteemed, eugenics is categorically at the center of the most abhorrent of all injustices, yet it is lauded as the ultimate "justice." How can this contorted mind-numbing ideology be good and "just"? How can it be construed or defined as "righteous"? An understanding of the historical foundations and mindset of eugenics provides an answer for how it has come to be embraced, and how it continues to wreak havoc on humanity even to this day.

As noted, Hitler embraced eugenics as he ruthlessly killed over six million Jews, and over 15 million others. His "justification" for evil acts during the Holocaust was fundamentally to eradicate all of whom he deemed "undesirables." The grand scheme (using Darwin's "survival of the fittest") inculcates the idea that a pure "master race" can be achieved if all those of undesirable lineage (people of different races who, they contend, pollute the gene pool) are eradicated. One of Hitler's sophomoric designs was to arbitrarily conduct rudimentary "caliper" tests; these tests were given to assess the broadness of one's nose. Nazi's believed broad-noses were symptomatic of ethnic inferiority, and therefore these people were deemed not worthy of life. In addition to over six million Jews, over three million Pols, over one million gypsies, there were several million more who were slaughtered because they were homosexuals or disabled! To prevent what he believed would further "taint" the gene pool, women were also forcibly sterilized! Does this sound "compassionate"? Is this representative of "women's rights" and justly justice?

While Hitler stands as example of an anathema to all humanity, he was actually heralded (by some) while he carried out his grotesque experimentation and genocidal "cleansing." As it turns out, Margaret Sanger (Planned Parenthood founder) applauded and was simpatico with Hitler and his acts of selective genocide that swept parts of Europe during the early 1900s.

While liberal/activists universally conveniently ignore the merits and accomplishments of the women's rights pioneer, Susan B. Anthony, they praise and applaud Margaret Sanger as the quintessential pioneer of women's rights. What's unmistakable and ironic though, is that Sanger, like Hitler, hated humanity and delighted in proliferating the most vile and grotesque forms of injustice. She was horribly bigoted and an admitted racist that possessed a keen desire to focus on the active elimination all Blacks and Hispanics through *the woman and her offspring*.

While evil clearly consumed her, Sanger is celebrated! Again, she is a noted "liberal" icon, and has been resoundingly touted by world dignitaries and heads of State. Contemporaries like Hillary

R. Clinton and Barack H. Obama tout Sanger as a quintessential American hero and "women's rights pioneer." That notwithstanding, an accurate view of Sanger's record and account is what provides undisputed truth as to the depth of her delusions and her contorted and contrived heart full of hatred. Some of Sanger's despicable acts include her actively participating as keynote speaker for the women's KKK rallies; following in the footsteps of the Democrats' brazen liberalism (regrettably, even present to this day) and the KKK as the enforcement–arm for their brand of "justice," Sanger was a frequent honored guest at KKK events and ceremonies. Sanger is applauded for being a thought-leader and trendsetter, but after reviewing some of her direct quotes, a better picture of the kind of person she was begins to emerge. Some direct quotes are summarized in the following:

> *"...we are paying for and even submitting to the dictates of an ever increasing, unceasingly spawning class of human beings who never should have been born at all"- Margret Sanger, "Pivot of Civilization"*
>
> *"The most merciful thing that a large family does to one of its members is to kill it"- Margaret Sanger.*
>
> *"We don't want the word to get out that we want to exterminate the Negro population"- Margaret Sanger.*
>
> *"The purpose of birth control was 'to create a race of thoroughbreds'..."Birth control must ultimately lead to a cleaner race"....- Margaret Sanger, Birth Control Review.*
>
> *"...human weeds," "...reckless breeders," "...unfit," "...feeble-minded" and "...undesirables"-* All terms Sanger used to describe and characterize Blacks (and Hispanics)
>
> *" more children from the fit, less from the unfit—that is the chief aim of birth control"- Sanger.*
>
> *"Blacks and Jews are a menace to the race...We must prevent multiplication of this bad stock...." Sanger.*

There are many more blatantly horribly evil quotes from Sanger, but they are far too many (and grotesque) to mention. The point is, how does the human mind and soul become so warped and demented that such creatures (like Sanger, Hitler, et. al.) are whitewashed from history to the point they become lauded and applauded?

Sanger's tireless commitment to eliminate Blacks was unrelenting. She focused on the Black community even to the point of paying Black pastors $100 for every sermon touting the "merits" of abortion over the pulpit! As outrageous as it sounds, this diabolical scheme was "masterfully successful"; many Black pastors relented and took the money. Regrettably, repercussions of this scheme are being felt even to this day! Sanger instituted what she called, "the Negro Project." The purpose of the project was to severely "reduce or eliminate" reproduction within the Black community. The American Birth Control League promoted this new program, Sanger and her fellow eugenics pushed it through so there would be African-American-led indoctrination, birth control policies and even sterilization throughout the U.S. Many states adopted forced sterilization programs for the "feeble-minded," incarcerated, and others deemed to be "unfit." Some of these programs still exist today under the guise of "compassion" and "justice." Does *any* of this seem "just"? Can it at all align with what he have confirmed and defined as "justly justice"?

As a result of Sanger's actions, in certain parts of the country there are more abortions in the Black community than live births! Numerous media outlets confirm that in New York, abortion of Black babies outnumber the live births of this same community at a rate of 55.8% (in 2014). Regrettably, this occurs while the newly elected mayor of N.Y gleefully lauds and applauds Planned Parenthood. Additional recent 2014 CDC reports confirm in Mississippi 72% of all babies aborted are Black babies. And in Georgia, the CDC confirms approximately 55% of all abortions are Black babies, and 80% of all abortions are "non-White." These sad statistics confirm abortion is being used exactly in the way Sanger intended, to reduce and/or eliminate Blacks (primarily); the “enlightened,” pseudo-intellectual-elitist types don’t bemoan it; they actually applaud and encourage it. The disproportional plight of Black and Hispanic communities should be alarming, especially after considering Sanger’s own words of wanting to eliminate “undesirables” (whom she deemed were Blacks and Hispanics). Her tactics were designed to mollify communities; she immediately began indoctrinating, using terms like “women’s health clinics” to put communities at ease. Planned Parenthood has successfully proliferated within urban settings and to this day overwhelmingly dominates as the number-one abortion provider within these fragile communities. There are many who will attempt to conveniently ignore and excuse the proliferation of abortion mills/clinics in these communities as happenstance and as natural forces of supply-and-demand, but actual facts and statistics preclude any of these excuses from serious consideration and rational thought

There are many grim facts and statistics about Sanger’s Planned Parenthood schemes that are quite illuminating and incontrovertible. For instance, while Planned Parenthood purposely conceals its actual office/data, there are some estimates that indicate up to 90% of all Planned Parenthood “clinics” are strategically located in Black communities. After confronted with these stats, Planned Parenthood tries to explain it away by stating they are altruistically providing “healthcare services” to Blacks. By just reflecting on Sanger’s own words, however, there’s confirmation of a duplicitous and conflicting agenda, as compared to the public persona of a “compassionate” and altruistic Planned Parenthood. More notable inconvenient facts actually help confirm Margret Sanger’s master plan of “elimination” is still alive and well, to be sure. Please consider these facts:

- Blacks make up only 13% of the entire U.S. population.
- Of the 13%, only approximately ½ are female (therefore able to bear children), which brings down the available Black “demographic” to approximately 6.5%.

- Of the entire female population, only one-half are of child-bearing age (approx. 15 to 44 years of age), which brings down the available Black demographic to approximately 3%!
- Of all abortions, approximately 40% are done to Blacks.
- While representing on a 3% demographic, Black babies make up approximately 23 million of the approximately 56 million abortions.

It's clear that for certain segments of society, the most dangerous place to be is in the womb; this connects the dots with the battle that has raged from the beginning (between good and evil), but this ought not to be! If good/God is to prevail, we must thwart these evil tactics that belie "*the woman and her offspring*." After considering the specific quotes and confirmed deeds of Margret Sanger, is it logical (in any way, shape or form) to believe Planned Parenthood is motivated purely by altruism and "justice" for women? Does it make any sense that a business would strategically locate the gross majority of their facilities (again approx. 90% by some estimates) into areas inhabited by a meager 3% of an available demographic? If they were sincere about proliferating services to every woman (without any regard or consideration of race) wouldn't it make more sense that we would see Planned Parenthood's located right next to every Walmart throughout America? Walmart already provides Planned Parenthood with demographic research, as they are a "magnet" for women as the key demographic, so why don't we see these "health clinics" next to Walmarts across America? Dr. Martin Luther King, Jr.'s niece, Alveda King, correctly assessed and characterized abortion as follows: "Abortion is the White supremacists best friend"! After recognizing the level of contrived evil with slave-owners and their abortive history, Hitler's history with eugenics, and now Margret Sanger's abhorrent history as an advocate for the KKK and eugenics, we see an indisputable connection! The sheer wisdom of Alveda King's quote becomes especially poignant.

As previously mentioned, the regrettable reality that results from not extending the basic human right to come forth and merely exist for the poorest and most needy among us, results in more deaths to Black children, more damage to Black women's bodies and more destruction to the Black community in general. The gross reality garnered from the aforementioned percentages confirms Planned Parenthood has adopted an eradication strategy (for Blacks/ "communities of color"), but they have succeeded in doing it in complete obscurity. To be sure, where are the protests? Where are the "racial justice" proponents and agencies? Where do NAACP and LaRaza stand when to comes to Planned Parenthood and its commitment to eugenics? Regrettably, they stand directly alongside of them! There should collective outrage appropriately pointing out this very real "war on women" (and "war on Blacks" for that matter), but conspicuously there is no outrage. To date, Margret Sanger and people of her ilk (social "elites," radical liberal/democrats and feminists) have succeeded in proliferating the deaths of over 56 million babies in the U.S. as a result of abortion, but again, where is the outrage? Is this "justly justice?" Why is this somehow palatable and acceptable? Digging even deeper into this issue will provide clarity and bring it full-circle!

Most people have grown to somehow accept not protecting the unborn; the most prevalent reasoning seems to be because exactly that, they are simply unborn! Until the advent of the sonogram and ultrasound technology, Bernard Nathanson, a well-known self-admitted abortionist also believed that preborn babies are not human beings. His mind changed when technology confirmed his worst nightmare, that life actually begins at conception. Upon this scientific confirmation, to his horror he had to admit (by his own estimates) he was responsible for killing approximately 75,000 unborn children. This realization shook him to his core, and he relented and repented and began telling the truth about abortion and his schemes to get it legalized (even to the extent to perjury) with many false testimonies to the Supreme court (in Roe v. Wade). Nathanson is also the mastermind of generating clichés and messaging that he and a male assistant thought could be used to manipulate and deceive women. Clever slogans and messaging like, "woman's right to choose," "freedom of choice," etc, are actually terms of manipulation and were cynically created by conniving men hoping to deceive and manipulate women; even to this day, these cynical slogans are heralded as the "holy grail" of womanhood! Does this seem right and "just"? At some point we need to arrive at just assessing evil deceivers by their word and deeds; the deeds of Sanger and strategies of Nathanson make it clear that the Planned Parenthood and Roe v. Wade decision (respectively) are schemes designed fundamentally to eliminate "undesirables"! They don't exist for justice; certainly not as we would define it. By definition they want to usher in and embolden the worst of gross injustice. The Supreme Court was used as a "supreme tool" to further the battle (between good and evil), as it took unprecedented actions to inordinately "tip the scales" in the direction of evil.

Our historical documents (Declaration of Independence and Constitution) make clear the guarantee of life, as a fundamental condition of "justice," yet a diabolical U.S. Supreme Court ceremoniously usurped it. During the Roe v Wade court case, they weighed the words and context of the 14th Amendment which states, "…nor shall any state deprive any person of *life,* liberty, or property, without due process of law, nor deny any person within its jurisdiction the equal protection of the law." With the utmost of temerity and to sheer disgust, the court declared it could not resolve when life begins, and on that basis gave a right to abortion based on the right to privacy. The court also admitted however, "if…personhood (for the unborn) is established, the appellant's case, of course, collapses, for the fetus' right to life is then guaranteed specifically by the (Fourteenth) Amendment." The courts were wrong, and conspired with the elites to confer the right to abortion without "just" justification. Even our ultra-progressive, liberal stalwart (and feminist) Supreme Court Justice Ruth Bader Ginsberg confirms the truth about abortion. She plainly states,

"Frankly, I had thought that at the time Roe was decided, there was concern about population growth, and particularly growth in populations that we don't want to have too many of." That's a true statement, from a true liberal feminist who staunchly supports Planned Parenthood! As a leader and die-hard Liberal Democrat, she understands eugenics and stands by every principle of its racist, bigoted underpinnings. With today's hypersensitivity about racism, why haven't we heard about justice Ginsberg making such absurd and "racist" statements? Why haven't popular shows that purportedly stand for "justice" and "women's issues" (like "The View," "Oprah" etc.) had lengthy shows and debates surrounding Ginsberg's comments and the respective outcomes targeted at the Black community? The only unfortunate answer we can conclude is that they are wholly complicit! Wouldn't shows committed to compassion and encouraging attributes of the beneficent resoundingly condemn Ginsberg and Sanger for their racial bigotry that results in horrible deaths of the innocent? Does Ginsberg's comments indicate support for racist eugenics-based schemes of the past? You bet it does! Most involved in this issue know the truth, but will cower behind evil ideology or a sliver of "science" to help mollify their sensibilities. Now, however, science is changing how abortion is viewed, and liberal mindsets are losing "cover."

With sophisticated technologies that have evolved over these past 40 years, we can definitively confirm when life begins and we can further confirm that babies do indeed feel pain in the womb. Importantly, we are now at a point in our history when scientists (based on available technology) can agree on the vital issue of "life."

Dr. Alfred M. Bongioanni, professor of pediatrics and obstetrics at the Univ. of Pennsylvania, states: "I have learned from my earliest medical educations that human life begins at the time of conception….I submit that human life is present throughout this entire sequence, from conception to adulthood, that that any interruption at any point throughout this constitutes a termination of human life…" He went on, "I am no more prepared to say that these early stages (of development in the womb) represent an incomplete human being that I would be to say that the child prior to the dramatic effects of puberty…is not a human being. This is human life at every stage." Professor, Hymie Gordon at the Mayo Clinic says, "by all the criteria of modern molecular biology, life is present from the moment of conception." Professor Micheline Matthews-Roth of Harvard University Medical School says, "it is incorrect to say that biological data cannot be decisive…It is scientifically correct to say that an individual human life begins at conception…Our laws, one function of which is to help preserve the lives of our people, should be based on accurate scientific data." It is quite interesting and noteworthy to observe how duplicitous leaders (primarily political) and prognosticators insist on demanding obedience to "science" when it comes to the issue of the environment and "global warming," but when it comes to "life" they are disgustingly quiet about assertions of scientific facts. They are notably motivated by expedience, not facts; further, they are cowards! Another professional Dr. Watson Bowes from the University of Colorado Medical School confirms, "the beginning of a single human life is from a biological point of view a simple and straightforward matter-the beginning is conception. This straightforward biological fact should not be distorted to serve sociological, political or economic goals." With all that been stated on the record (beginning with the Bible, slave owners, genocidal maniacs, Sanger, Supreme Court Justice Ginsberg, and now with doctors and scientists), it is unequivocally confirmed that as a matter of scientific, pragmatic and humanitarian fact *that only justly justice is real justice that embraces life for all humankind beginning at conception*!

Stubborn mindsets are hard to overcome. If statements from Sanger, and doctors and scientists still don't appropriately satisfy *any* lingering doubts about the veracity of the sacredness of life and when it begins, listen to Planned Parenthood (itself) as it truthfully confirms that abortion *kills life*! In its own document, Planned Parenthood states, "an abortion kills the life of a baby after it has begun." It is *dangerous to your life and health.*" Now, is this *really* indicative of "women rights"? It went on to say, "It may make you sterile, so that when you want a child you cannot have it…"~ Planned Parenthood pamphlet entitled "Plan Your Children." It also confirms, "one sperm plus one egg = one baby"~ Planned Parenthood pamphlet entitled "ABC's of Birth Control." Is the picture of manifest evil becoming clearer? Can people who are serious about standing for "justice" and "women's rights" logically support Planned Parenthood with its well-documented evil machinations to specifically target the *women and her offspring*? If we are completely honest and truthful with ourselves, we would clearly confirm that the Liberals' battle-cry about the "war on women" does exist; instead of it being waged by another political party or "the religious right" (as liberals would portend), it is indeed being waged at the hand of Margaret Sanger's Planned Parenthood! We can't have it both ways, and there is definitively no two ways around realization of the level of gross dereliction by Planned Parenthood.

What is the definition of *to kill* or *to murder*? A quick search of both these terms confirms the accurate definition is *to take someone's life*. This begs the question, has our conscience become so debased and maligned by lies that we can no longer feel, sense or understand brazenly murderous acts? If for some reason our conscience has been seared to the extent we will not fight for the right to merely exist (as a matter of 1st principle), will we at least commit to fight in God's battle for "*the woman and her offspring*" as a matter of 1st principle? We have verified that there is an epic battle between good and evil, that indeed evil exists and persists, and it wants to undermine and consume all humanity! What will we do about it? Will we uncompromisingly stand with and for Godliness and goodness, while ardently fighting against evil? Or will we somehow betray our own stated "justice" principles and cower to evil?

This chapter was quite a ride! We uncovered eugenics, Margaret Sanger and her evil schemes precipitated through Planned Parenthood, and we heard from doctors and scientists about when life begins. This presented a great opportunity for uncovering the real battle and the real intent of those who purport justice, but use the term to garner sympathy and support without any intent or desire to bring about justice by standing by the basic right to exist. This culminates in a great conundrum!

The Declaration of Independence declares that all have the unalienable right to *life, liberty, and pursue happiness*. While this is a clear an unequivocal declaration, it has now unfortunately come to mean that 'I have the right to be happy regardless of whom I injure." We must now must face ourselves and seriously ask very difficult questions of ourselves about the ramifications of this new knowledge. We must ask ourselves, Do we really understand and embody the fact that the only way to begin healing and transforming communities requires holding "life" with primacy (as 1st principle) while shunning support of any unjust people, parties, charismatic personalities, traditions, etc.? After hearing their own words of support for Planned Parenthood, abortion, etc., will we confront the unjust with truth? Will we allow clergy of *any* religions to hide behind empty platitudes like "social justice," "racial justice" and "human rights" while supporting organization (or people) opposed to providing the basic and essential human right these distinctions purportedly stand for? Will we remain quiet and therefore complicit while the battle between good and evil rages, and while God wants to use us to intervene on behalf of *"the woman and her offspring"*? Will we vote for *any persons* who are not definitively justly just? Lastly, will we finally stand for something, or perpetually relegated to gross cowardice languishing in our own vile hypocrisy? Hypocrisy is upon us, so if we are going to end injustice at all, we must stand!

Chapter Seven

"HIPPOCRATIC OATH"/HYPOCRITICAL OAF

"Just because you cannot fight every evil does not mean you should fight no evils."

~ Dennis Prager

By now, empirical facts should provide us the ability to agree and unify on the premise that "justice begins in the womb"! By definition then, Social Justice begins in the womb! Also, Racial Justice begins in the womb! And, Human Rights begins in the womb! For those truly committed to justice in any form, the root of our cause begins with perpetuating justice as it is conceived in the womb. Again, only this is real justly justice! Justly Justice is the only viable stand as it is perfectly aligned and congruent with its self-defined objective. It is a strategic distinction necessary to move forward because it is the fundamental elemental basis for reconciling ***all*** justice movements, ***all*** justice-focused people and organizations, and ***all*** Faiths into one unified movement! Who could've imagined that committing to real justice just based on "life"/existence would make it easier to comprehend and therefore achieve. That's exactly what it does. As long as we are principled, a commitment to a standard of justly justice actually makes achieving justice "easy"!

James Bond is famous for his "shaken not stirred" preferences for his martinis. As we've progressed through the book you are probably experiencing being both shaken *and stirred*! All should be shaken and stirred by the pronounced magnitude of unfettered sheer injustice running rampant in America and around the world. What should be particularly galling is the amount of injustice perpetuated at the hand of those proclaiming "justice"! If you are like me, by this point, you have already dutifully repented for having unwittingly supported and/or participated (in any way) in the worst and most vile human scourge in history of mankind. If you haven't felt compelled to do so yet, no worries! There is still more to cover, so perhaps as we move along, an appropriate degree of contrition and repentance will occur as we press down on and press further into these timely issues.

At this point, many will either wholly embrace gross hypocrisy or stand for justly justice! If we truly stand for truth, righteousness and justice, we cannot be double-minded; we will love and uphold one standard of justice (based on 1st principles and justly justice), while hating even the slightest of deceptions from the other. Or, we will continue to mindlessly herald and uphold dutifully hypocritical oaths to nebulous distinctions (like, social justice, racial justice, and human rights) while rejecting humanity's most needy!

All doctors take an Hippocratic oath, swearing to practice medicine wisely, uphold all medical standards, and as a matter of 1st principle " they commit to "*first, do no harm.*" In the same vein, based on what we have uncovered about the vital issues of justice, an oath is now ours to take. In order to be truly effective moving forward, people who stand for justice, or more accurately justly justice, must commit to an oath to "*first, allow to exist.*" If we take a Hippocratic oath-type stand, we will stave off labels and accusations connoting a litmus test or purest tests for "justice." The fact is there is no litmus test; it's a reality check! The reality is, if we're sincere about justice, the most basic way we show it is to allow another to merely exist. We cannot sincerely begin to reconcile America and all the factions therein until we unite and reconcile behind the truth. Our pledge is not to a litmus test, it is to a profound principle of upholding righteousness in order to restore us (individually and collectively) to a righteous people not content with living in contorted hypocrisy.

There's nothing impractical or mysterious about life, it's just the simple matter-of fact reality that confirms common sense and basic human decency! Likewise, it is also a fundamental factor in the battle for God. For those who want to be used by/for God in His Kingdom battle (and for His divine purposes), they must fundamentally commit to His creation and allow it to come forth! Again, there's no litmus or purity test; complete alignment with the truth and reality is the *only* way to sincerely and irreproachably express our desire for and our commitment to justly justice without hypocrisy. Hypocrisy is a huge impediment to a successful movement; it completely disempowers. The bottom line is, hypocrisy not only wholly disempowers, it is the primary factor that breeds disunity and contempt.

The dawning of a new time, new season, and a new day is upon us. Perversions of thoughts, ideas and persuasions are leaving. Hypocrisy is on the run and unity is culminating into a new beginning. We will no longer relegate ourselves as willing vessels that inculcate falsehoods; we will stand for truth and righteousness. People are again turning their hearts to righteousness and truth and justly justice is one the rise. Do you perceive it?

Irrespective to debased mindsets expressing liberality while pressing with continual drumbeats and mantras demonizing all others about a purported "war on women," the fact is, people's eyes are opening and the dawning of a new day has begun. The latest polls show a perceptible increase in the commitment to "life"; now, majorities of over 62% of all Americans are "pro-life" and fully understand life begins at conception! This is great news and quite an improvement, but it also still shows there are a committed number of people (approx. 38%) who have not yet come to know or accept facts about "life." It also means that, irrespective as to how compelling the facts are, many will still allow themselves to be used as "tools" and agents of evil as opposed to weapons for good. Because of what can be characterized as acute "soul sickness," many hurting souls will always look to breach or impeach God's divine authority over all His humanity. Instead of a commitment to protect life, they will still look to defile and reject *existence* as it attempts to come forth from the "*woman and her offspring*." This is where the battle started and this is where it must culminate and be ardently defended!

Specious arguments, liberal grandiosity and unfettered pomposity, has primacy in the radical liberals' mindset; but, even with their strategic obfuscations, there is no mistaking that the tactics used by these treacherous souls have led the way to utter destruction of the most needy of humankind. Regrettably though, through brazenly hypocritical stances and the lack of knowledge and truth that would've allowed us to hold people accountable, we've allowed people who wholly embrace untenable lies and falsehoods to perpetuate the overlaying of scourge upon the least and most vulnerable. This is a crying shame!

If these revelations have moved you to the extent it has affected me, you sense now is a time and season to repent and relent. With broken and contrite hearts, now is a great time to pray; here is my simple prayer: "*Lord, I repent for unknowingly participating in the epic battle that rages against You and Your creation. I relent my preconceived notions, idols and ideology by placing them all at Your feet and throne as a sacrifice. I ask that You replace them all with Your divine nature and 1st principles.*"

For those who are "souled-out" (relatively speaking, embracing a stricken soul), this simple prayer may not have an effect. All is not lost however because at the very least it should give impetus and prompt us go deeper into our most pressing confrontation. The confrontation of "self"!

With what has been factually uncovered about our respective history and the truths thereof, a permanent change of direction for the wise and prudent is the only acceptable response. Questions that should persist at the moment are, "how can officials portend to stomp for justice while undermining it completely? Why isn't 'leadership' held fully accountable for human atrocities happening to the most innocent?" The answer is, most of those in leadership are first and foremost committed to fundraising for their agency, and/or empowering a social/political platform; they are not committed to "justice" (certainly not the justice we've confirmed and defined). Many willfully proliferate incoherent drivel, and look to propagandize the masses of the willfully ignorant (or as Lenin describes, "the useful idiots"). But, is this really who we've become? Will we continue to remain complicit while watching millions die every year? Are we willing to lose the principled constructs of our very soul for populist messages and clever marketing, and to just stand with cowards unwilling to stand up for actual poor, helpless, and least among us? If so, we've committed to a life's stand for what can only be described as a hypocritical oaf!

Hypocritical oafs are those who has no real tenor in the soul. They are tossed to and fro, and are completely unmoored from core principles or reality! These people have indeed thrown in with the slave owners and Marxist/Socialist/Communist genocidal dictators of the past, while aligning with the "Margaret Sangers" of the present, all under the pretext of "justice." Unfortunately, they have been masterfully manipulated and used as formidable tools to increase the stench of a profane and debased humanity devoid of compassion for the least and most needy among us! Fundamentally, embracement of the mindset of a hypocritical oaf is dangerous because it connotes a rejection of reality; it purposes to have facts bent and contorted to fit the world as it imagined, not as it really is. A hypocritical oaf lives a life that horribly suffers from gross self-deception, but instead of recognizing it and intervening by asking for help and seeking truth, the oaf relishes in deception!

Of all deceptions, the most vile and unrelenting type of deception is self-deception; it is an insatiable slave-master hell-bent on consuming the soul in an inescapable web of lies! Self-deception makes people slaves to their own heart and soul, as it continuously wrangles and contorts reality. Depending on the level of deception(s), it is difficult or impossible to confront. It cannot be satisfied because it always resolves itself in a viscous cycle of circuitous lies. Further, it produces a "heart of lies" and perpetually subjugates the soul to false "realities" and contrived mindsets. Self-deception is important to note because it is the principality that confounds "the wise" about the basic issue of "life," thus making them "fools."

Other than self-deception, all other types of deceptions and acts of deceit can be dealt with when confronted. Typically, when we can ask person(s) who have wronged us to apologize and request recompense for deceptive acts committed toward us, we can (in most cases) be made "whole." Self-deception has no such constructs. It is wholly empowered by us, it thrives in and on us (in our very soul) and it is relentless at destroying us! The destruction caused by self-deception is what produces horrible liars. Additionally, it produces masters of contradictions and hypocrisy. Notably, it completely defiles!

Regrettably, some egregious examples of self-deception and hypocrisy can be expressed on an institutional basis, and can be found in many parishes, churches and synagogues. Many churches/denominations lose membership as people walk from away from any formal religious or spiritual activities, because of what they view as having experienced gross contradictions. When definitive proclamations are espoused and preached (like sacredness of life, for instance), yet not wholly followed or adhered to, parishioners may tend to leave. Gross hypocrisy has been noted as one of the primary reasons many lose faith. One way to restore creditability and Holy authority is to adhere to the simple 1st principle of "life." All other Godly admonitions can best established and adhered to if they flow from this unequivocal 1st principle. Let's illustrate by asking some basic questions: How can Churches or Faith institutions purport to care for the poor, if they reject the notion that the poorest among us is in the womb?

How can Faith organizations tout the need for "racial"/equality, while seemingly rejecting the basic right to life while it targets specific race(s)? How can organizations raise the specter of racial discrimination, while ignoring the facts about the disproportional plight of Blacks (and Hispanics) as they are strategically aborted? How can churches endorse and support political parties/politicians/institutions simply because of "race" or because an assertion, "I will do anything, if I can just save one life, one child...," while (in reality) they wholly embrace the purposeful elimination of entire segments of children? When parishioners see religious institutions endorse and tout people/politicians who manifest a wholly antithetical mindset to the Bible, they sense the institution has a commitment to hypocrisy and expediency, not an uncompromising stand for righteousness and truth!

The Bible coupled with common sense and common decency dictate the issue of life should be central to *any* faith organizations or agencies. Since the battle between good and evil culminates with, *"the woman and her offspring,"* this issue should take primacy! Yet, an untold number of "faith" organizations (churches or otherwise) wholly adopt mindsets based on their respective "livelihood" and community influence while forsaking the livelihood of the most innocent and the most poor among us! A prime example of this can been seen with Rev. Jesse Jackson. In the early to mid 1970s, before Jesse Jackson first ran for president, he correctly assessed Planned Parenthood and their strategies to eliminate "undesirables" (a Sanger term), as "Black genocide" (Jet magazine 1973); he coined this term, and he was correct! In 1975, Jackson joined Ruth Graham (wife of Billy Graham) in support of a Constitutional Amendment to ban abortion. In 1980 Jackson compared abortion to slavery. In 1984, when he announced he was running for president of the United States, however, he radically changed his stance, and became pro-abortion, wholly supporting Planned Parenthood even as it ravaged the very communities he purportedly committed his life's work to help strengthen and save. We can surmise such a radical shift took place in order to raise funds while launching his Democratic presidential campaign, and to buttress his respective foundations (Rainbow/PUSH coalition, etc.)! This demonstrates a total rejection of Jackson's principles and commitment for the community in order to garner support and consolidate unto himself money/power/influence from diabolical political and social "masterminds."

Anyone possessing common decency and basic sensibilities would view Jesse Jackson's acts of hypocrisy and contradiction as most appalling. We must ask ourselves, will we now begin to hold self-described civil rights leaders like Jesse Jackson and Al Sharpton culpable for their firm commitment to Black genocide via their strident support of eugenicists like Sanger/Planned Parenthood? Will we reject these people for their complete disregard for justly justice? Since there is overwhelming evidence of grotesque support for killing of innocents, incredulity on our part is not an adequate response. Only complete rejection and disavowing support for these individuals and their respective organizations should suffice for people committed to justly justice.

As we see, rejection of basic core tenets of human decency can be easily dismissed if there is gross self-deception. Many have been bought and fully paid for with "special interests," promises of campaign donations, influence within political/Party structures, etc. As previously noted, even with mounds of evidence confirming the racist/bigoted machinations of foundations of Margaret Sanger and Planned Parenthood, both Hillary Clinton and Barack Obama wholly laud, applaud and endorse them and all aspects of recklessly ending the life of the most innocent (even through to "late-term"!). Under the guise of "women's rights," both Clinton and Obama have spoken at Planned Parenthood "celebrations" and gala events while touting Margaret Sanger and Planned Parenthood as institutions of "justice." While proudly receiving the Margaret Award in 2009, Hillary R. Clinton gushed, "I admire Margaret Sanger enormously, her courage, her tenacity, her vision…taking on archetypes, taking on attitudes and accusations flowing from all directions I am really in awe of her." Based on grotesque actions to align with noted evil, how can these people assert themselves as advocates for justice? Based on their abhorrent mindset and purposeful actions, how can they have any creditability, following or support?

It used to be when someone stood on the shoulder of historical racist miscreants, and walked "arm-in-arm" with verifiable racists, they themselves would be correctly deemed as racists. What happened to equally applying these standards? Do they not apply to certain people because of their political party/ideology or backgrounds? Why aren't people held accountable for their gross dereliction and deemed (at best) "racialists" who take advantage of race-based strategic manipulations, or at worst racists like those eugenicist/agencies whom they have pledged their lives to follow (e.g. Hitler and Sanger)? Does this mean by definition that our current president (Obama) and presidential candidate (Hillary Clinton) are tools of injustice? Does it mean, based on their unabashed support of Sanger/Planned Parenthood, self-professed civil rights "leaders" (like Jesse Jackson and Al Sharpton) along with media (New York Times, MSNBC, NBC, CBS, ABC, Hollywood/actors), and purported agencies of justice (like NAACP, Congressional Black Caucus, LaRaza, SPLC) are actually vehicles that proliferate injustice?

The fact is, there are many people and organizations primarily committed to ideology and therefore ignore reality via constructs of self-deception. Regrettably, because of money and influence they actively promote people/political parties/organizations who are by definition ardently anti-life and proliferate the worst of injustices in the battle for *"the woman and her offspring."*

Do we continue headlong with embracing ideology that makes us hypocritical oafs? How can one purport to be "liberal" and enlightened, while supporting the worst barbaric scourges known to man? In all honesty, does this seem enlightened? Why is it excused while politicians, actors, musicians, and "leaders" (of any sort) are heralded and left unscathed for their detachment from real "justly justice"? Our collective dereliction and veritable reprobation on this issue has allowed the U.S. to accelerate far beyond the Hitler's horrors of killing over six million Jews. We've continued the demonic legacy hatched from the beginning of man, by attaching new words like eugenics, women's rights and other mantras, to justify killing almost 60 million more people (10 times the number attributed to Hitler); we're doing this even after vowing "never again"! Our current path confirms we have collectively lost our souls! Only a commitment to 1st principles (a "Hippocratic oath" of sorts) will allow us to regain our "compass" on justly justice, while fighting fervently against *all* injustice. But as we've uncovered in this chapter, self-deception runs deeply and cannot be easily "cured," as it constantly self-corrects in a diaspora of elaborately ornate (yet archaic) web of lies. This can leave churches/synagogues/parishes, as well as organizations, political parties and entire communities victims of gross and brazen hypocrisy. The question is, will we perpetually succumb to being hypocritical oafs, or will we reject the subtle manipulations of our very souls to embrace 1st principles of righteousness truth and justice?

There is still more truth to uncover and actual work to do in coming up with solutions for clearly identifying justly justice while irreproachably standing for just causes. Embracement of deceptions and defending the illogical and indefensible are the enemies of real justice. The worst of deceptions emanate from recesses of our soul and spirit, so before we can assert a permanent shift in mindset and change of our worldview to uphold 1st principles of justly justice, there would need to be an "intervention" that will help definitively and permanently sever well-entrenched "soul-ties." To accomplish this, we will need a heaping helping of "soul food"; "food" that is designed to nourish and replenish our very soul!

Chapter Eight

SOUL FOOD

Nourishment for the misaligned soul

"Virtue cannot separate itself from reality without becoming a principle of evil."

~ Albert Camus

If we are to make progress toward real justly justice, we must become astute in matters of the soul and spirit; we must firmly understand their impact on our understanding and on our individual actions.

Throughout this book, there has been continuous building and uncovering of a plethora of new historical facts and truths. Most of these truths have been strategically veiled and whitewashed from our history by revisionists who have allowed heinous acts to occur under relative obscurity. Since most have gone unnoticed and unchecked, we can now see there has been purposeful manipulation by unaccountable duplicitousness of agendas driven by manifest hypocrisy. To be sure, there are examples of several of the most notorious masterminds in world history who have entered the annals of history heralded as "pioneers" and "innovators of justice," when in actuality they should be universally despised and rejected as pariahs. How did this happen? A simplistic answer is, we have entered into an era very strongly ruled by principalities of deception(s) and therefore we cannot discern truth and righteousness. Many have come to reject sound doctrine and fundamental truths as "evil," and have learned to call evil "good"!

Isaiah 5:20 warns of these times. It declares, "Woe to those who call evil good and good evil, who put darkness for light and light for darkness, who put bitter for sweet and sweet for bitter." Wow! Take a moment to seriously read and contemplate this warning and admonition. Isn't this exactly symptomatic of the myriad issues discussed in this text? This verse confirms that what we are currently experiencing is not new. Our current societal plight is a symptomatic of a continuous paradigm that has occurred in cycles since the beginning of man! Evil is celebrated as good, while good is abhorred and rejected as evil. Isaiah warns and admonishes so people will begin to open their eyes and observe; once people can make observation, they can begin to shift and correct. "Shifting" would seem obvious and rather simple, but in reality this is exceptionally hard for those whose souls have been pierced and laden with falsehoods at the core of their innermost being. The biggest and lasting shifts that will take us from accepting generic platitudes portending "justice", to a committed stance for real justly justice, must take place in the realm of the spirit.

While many people will be able to make an immediate shift based on new facts, knowledge and truth, there are far too many who will remain stubbornly unchanged; this complicates and prolongs the momentum and acceleration of cultural and societal changes to the firm commitment of justly justice. Unrelenting attacks targeted at *"the woman and her offspring"* require we take immediate additional steps to bring along even the most ardent of naysayers to the side of justly justice. For these however (ardent naysayers), self-deception is strong. "Die-hards" won't allow themselves to receive radical shifts in perspective that take place in the knowledge realm (the "mind"); because of relative strongholds, they will only experience shifts taking place at deeper levels of the core of our being, in the spirit. Necessary interventions and shifts that displace strongholds and truly sets the captive free, must take place in the realm of the "spirit."

Before pressing into inner-workings and specific actions or interventions directed at the realm of the spirit, we should be really clear that those who stridently deny the right of existence for all mankind embody hypocritical and completely illogical ideology that's in desperate need of appropriate intervention. To help identify this syndrome using an acronym, we could say they are "HI" (hypocritical and illogical). Too many are living the "HI"-life; their life is dominated by self-deception, and they see life through a lens that is hypocritical, illogical and indefensible. Because it is relatively easy to dissociate when these things are discussed at a high level and without specific examples, there is need for specific examples that help produce observation of a few ever-present oxymoronic conundrums we face. While there are countless examples of pervasive mindsets dominating the "HI"-life, here are just a few examples that help illustrate people who have been getting "HI":

- You are HI if outraged over racism, while wholly supporting all the racist foundations (and current tactics) of Planned Parenthood.
- You are HI if you decry perceived "hate" precipitated by other races, while actually hating other races and income groups (like Whites and the "wealthy").
- You are HI if you rage about the need to extend welfare benefits/WIC programs, while actually helping to eliminate women, infants and children through support of Planned Parenthood as it targets these very segments.
- You are HI if you advocate "women's rights", while wholly supporting schemes targeted at harming women's bodies and eliminating their children.
- You are HI if you stand for God/Faith and religiosity, while fighting and battling on the side of evil as it targets the woman and her offspring!
- You are HI if you enshrine pictures, photos, in church/pulpits of people who are ardently pro-abortion, while at the same time purporting to stand for justice and God's righteous standards.

- You are HI to express outrage over income inequality, while standing with those who deny the basic equality for all of humanity to just exist.
- When unions/union bosses demand "workers rights" while proudly standing on the shoulders (historically) of slave owners, genocidal maniacs, eugenicists, and Margaret Sanger by denying the right of mankind to exist, they are HI! Ninety percent of Unions' political donations go to groups/politicians of this mindset.
- Religious organizations are HI when they march for, endorse and support (in any way) any political Parties, candidates or agencies who battle for evil in undermining God's divine plans for His creation.
- When churches/synagogues/parishes stand with any political Party apparatus as that denies God's Word, decimates and undermines Gods creation, and tacitly (or emphatically) embraces the evisceration of the poorest, most needy, most helpless among us (the unborn), they are HI!
- If any religious organization/institution supports Obamacare with its fundamental requirement supplanting religious rights and associated freedoms, and its demands of complete obedience (not to God, but to the government), they are HI!
- You are HI if you are a person committed to justice while wholly supporting in local, state (legislators and governor), and national (president and congress) elections, people who channel and enthrone the vile injustice of rejecting the right to simply exist.
- You are HI if you herald and applaud Bill Clinton (a person definitively guilty of predatory sexual perversions and behaviors) as a Party statesman and spokesman for civil/ "women's rights."

- You are HI to support rantings of purported claims of "injustice" from New York Times, MSNBC, NBC, "The View" and various journalists/actors/singers/performers (including Oprah, Jon Stewart, etc..), as they stand firm against the right to exist for the poorest, most put-upon and most innocent!
- People are HI to rant about "war on the poor" while these very same people are stalwarts for eugenics and Planned Parenthood, and are wholly committed to furthering the elimination of nearly 60 million babies (the poorest among us)!
- You are HI to stand for "open borders," while completely ignoring the plight of men, women and children being maimed and/or killed (over 10,000 deaths/year) by human/drug traffickers because of our unsecured borders!
- You are HI to claim that the death penalty for the worst of convicted felons who have been pronounced guilty is inhumane (because they may feel pain while dying), while fully supporting abortion in spite of scientific facts proving innocent babies (in the womb) feel excruciating pain while being aborted!
- You are HI if you give credence and support for any assertions that an ID card requirement is a "racist" tactic, while knowing full-well an ID card is required to: buy cigarettes, check cashing, library cards, driving automobile, flying on plane, getting a prescription, applying for Federal government assistance, being allowed to enter any Federal Government building, applying for a job, purchasing a car, donating blood, applying for Social Security services, and enrolling in ObamaCare (including prescriptions and Doctors' visits)! If rules of objectivity and consistency were applied, we would have to say all these mechanisms are racist, and the "chief racist" would have to be the President

(since all of these are either directly or indirectly influenced by him)!

- You are HI if you condemn others as "bigoted" simply because they share the exact same stance about traditional marriage as former President Bill Clinton, Hillary Clinton and President Obama before they "evolved" (over the past two years). Since the homosexual "evolution" of the Clintons and Barack Obama, all others are now deemed homophobic and bigoted if they share the "pre-evolution" mindset! This begs the question, Were the Clintons and President Obama homophobic and bigoted before their respective evolution?

- You are HI if you ignore the fact that homosexuals are rejected, abused, maimed, and killed in Muslim countries without a word from the President. Yet in the U.S., Christians who perform no such acts against homosexuals are resoundingly castigated and demonized for just attempting to uphold their Biblical beliefs.

Again, there are countless examples of living life on the HI. Truth be told, most of America has been getting HI, and actually for most of my life I was also HI. I was fully indoctrinated into Liberal/Progressive mindsets and was committed to voting based strictly on tradition; regrettably, I also fully participated in the mindset that encouraged destruction of life. After purposeful introspection, I realized that my mindset and stances were abhorrent and indefensible. In review of the HI's, we can now see there are many of our current stances that are utterly indefensible. Even with just the few aforementioned examples, did you observe any hypocrisy? Did you scoff? Were you somehow taken aback? Most importantly, did you observe how we are programmed to attempt to cure "injustice" (through rants, demonization, characterizations, etc.) while wholly embracing the *base* injustice impacting all mankind that ignores or rejects the 1st principle of "life"/existence? One of biggest challenges we must understand

and learn to embody is there can be no legitimate claims of "injustice" while supporting the worst of all "injustices"; this is oxymoronic and completely incoherent. Contrary to rhetoric and hyperbole, we can't have it both ways. Again, in all wisdom, Dr. Martin Luther King, Jr. exclaimed, "Injustice anywhere is a threat to justice everywhere." In other words, all injustice is injustice; *every one of the aforementioned examples completely rejects what can be defined as justly justice*!

With concerted effort, we can finally break the chain of perpetual hypocrisy in order to restore honor and integrity to our respective justice causes and ourselves. The everyday examples of pervasive mindsets pinpoint how we are complicit with our current plight; regrettably we've precipitated our current condition by supporting and empowering the wrong people (or agencies) with the wrong ideas. The levels of dereliction and prejudice, however, run deep, so interventions needed to help remedy our plight are not found in the realm of the soul where we process logic, reason and facts. This level of committed dereliction is only found and adequately remedied in the realm of the spirit.

Over 20 years ago, I was certified as an "Ontological Coach." That training coupled with life experiences allowed me to fully appreciate how ontological coaching can be used to produce core personal shifts in the human ontology so outcomes are exponentially more efficient and predictably better. Significant work in the realm of mind, body and spirit is how most interpersonal shifts take place. Many times, just helping people better observe these distinctions and their respective roles in shaping us, produces life-altering results! If there are acute strongholds, however, we must go beyond just improving the capacity for observation; we must intently intervene while working in the realm of the specific domains (mind, body, spirit).

While the best practice for ontological coaching is in-person, there are some practical shifts that can be made just through writing. Without belaboring a holistic understanding of mind, body and spirit and their respective complexities and interactions, in simple terms, it can be characterized in simple terms that these three domains work together to help define individuals at the core of their being. All actions (or lack thereof) are initiated out of all, multiple or just one of these domains. Since most of our actions happen automatically (when we're triggered, we act), knowing who you are and what you represent at the core of your being is paramount.

At the core of our being, there can be acute soul-ties and spirit-ties, and they are not equivalent. It is noteworthy to recognize that strongholds of the soul-where mind, will and emotions reside-can more easily be modified with new understand and truth. But strongholds of the spirit require much more rigor and additional attention, as these strongholds are exceptionally resilient and heavily motivated by subtleties of "moods."

Powerful convictions are mostly housed in the realm of the spirit; the spirit is where our pervasive moods live. If these moods are strong, they will override mind (soul realm) and body, and immediately propel us into action out of our very spirit! For example, if there are very strong pervasive moods about racism, and someone asserts it has occurred, it doesn't matter how many facts or verifiable logic are presented to the contrary, the mood will trigger a definitive action. This is best observed and understood when we consider that those who are against Obama Administration policies (generally) are castigated as "racist." If people align with the mindset of being Taxed Enough Already (TEA party mindset) and want smaller government, they are demonized as "racist." Those who want to decrease debt/deficits from the back of future generations of children and grandchildren are resoundingly characterized as "racist." As these caricatures are continuously replayed, many segments of society come to firmly accept them as absolute truth, and a stronghold is permanently rooted and enthroned!

There is now a hypersensitivity to racism, and manipulative masterminds recognize it. These nefarious, diabolical characters continually throw out the "race card" to neutralize and silence opposition, while ginning-up emotions of those gullible and hypertensive to the issue of race. It is to the point that even if facts are discovered that contradict the initial racist assertion, people with strong "spirit-ties" characterized by race moods will produce denials (even self-deception) to hold onto the pervasive mood that has been allowed fester in the spirit. This is what has systematically happened to large segments of the American culture. Nefarious masterminds infiltrate our best intentions and good nature to masterfully use/abuse the deep realms of our spirit; they know how to actually manipulate segments of the population into supporting people or causes that may be actually be fighting against their own (respective) best interests! Unless effective intervention of the soul and spirit take place, throngs of people will continue to be blinded by passions of the heart while being gripped and swept into complicit submission to manipulative deeds and agendas of others.

For centuries, cultures with intense histories of horrible evil, atrocities and wrongs (like African Americans, for instance), just the insinuation of racism and/or Whites abusing "the system" and taking advantage of "the people" produces community-wide rage and calls of injustice. Since history confirms patterns of gross injustice, there may be good reason to be cautious toward others, but what is so insidious about this tactic is that it doesn't necessarily have to be true! It just has to be posited by a "community leader" or someone in a leadership position (political/party, church, organization, media, etc.) and it is wholly accepted and immediately embodied as truth. This happens because the pervasive mood bypasses the mind, will and emotions (governed in the soul), and prominently imbeds itself in the realm of the spirit. Through the use of powerful imagery (via complicit "media"/outlets), and use of generalized caricatures (ascribing and asserting ungrounded labels on segments of people), Liberal

Progressives have become masterful at using these tactics to manipulate elections, alter the culture and silence all opposing voices and views. Their tactics work because through recurrent themes, they focus on producing powerful pervasive moods in the realm of the spirit. Once rooted, these moods are unwittingly enthroned and embodied as "truth."

With these examples, there should be more clarity about how American society has devolved to the point where it has become hypersensitive, polarized, insular, and balkanized. Issues pertaining to "racism," "war on women," "social justice," "immigration," etc., are hyped and manipulated in order to produce emotions like collective outrage, while most talking points surrounding these issues belie our best interests toward real justly justice; and far too often these stories are manifestly untrue! There has been a severe erosion of civility and tolerance, and most often "strongholds" (especially those in the realm of the spirit) are to blame.

We can overcome strongholds in the realm of the spirit by first recognizing they exist, then with purposeful and intense introspections of our heart seek to destroy them so purity and truth can again emanate from the core of our being. If we find that even with the plethora of information, facts and findings that has been uncovered, if we still have a penchant to defend people/agencies/ideology antithetical to justly justice, we would be emblematic of suffering from acute strongholds of the spirit. There is no doubt that many of us need to seek further help and make a serious commitment to prayer about this; willingly defending brazen ideology that rejects life of the poor and most innocent is something that only God can heal. He will only help us heal, though, as we seriously and intensely seek Him about it!

It should be noted, most often strongholds don't necessarily have us; we willingly come to the point of steadfastly embracing and embodying them! The realization that strongholds of the soul and spirit are typically characterized as unusually strong "soul-ties" that we unwittingly come to enthrone, is in itself an observation that will help break manipulative mindsets that have gripped and crippled our soul and spirit. It should now be quite apparent how manifestation of strong "soul-ties" can disempower individuals to the extent they virtually enslave themselves through steadfast commitment to untoward mindsets, traditions, ideologies, etc.

In one of my prior books, I characterized this paradigm as "Instanity." Instanity is a hybrid word that connotes a complicit heart that relishes in channeling an "instant," willful, purposeful cycle of "insanity"! The reaction to this chapter will confirm the level or degree of our willful instanity. If it prompts people to become angry or perturbed, and (irrespective of the preponderance of truth) redoubles the commitment to act in same ways they always have, they are a great example of instanity. If it illuminates, and causes contrition to the extent that one commits to no longer (under any circumstance) support *any* form of injustice, and especially the most blatant that belies existence to the most innocent, then progress is being made!

In summary, this chapter was designed to help confirm why so many can be deceived to the extent they support people or agencies that stand in complete opposition to their beliefs, and are antithetically aligned with their respective Faith. What has been uncovered is that a simplistic method of just providing people with more "information" is most often not going to solve the conundrum of people supporting hypocritical and illogical policies and agendas. Some people like to get HI, and relish in it! Proper intervention will need to effectively pierce deeper recesses of the inner being; just providing new tools to educate "low-information" segments of society is not necessarily the most effective tactic. To be most effective, strategies need to be developed that will help penetrate the realm of the spirit. Entrenched strongholds go well beyond the level of basic logic and rationality; they reside in the realm of the spirit where pervasive moods dominate and override the mind. The good news is, once these rather complex issues are brought forward and observed, effective actions to mitigate and permanently reduce their grip can be implemented. A concerted effort to commit to justly justice can only be achieved if all people will sincerely commit to introspection in the realms of the soul and spirit in order to overcome deep-rooted sentiments that can blind and preclude from strict adherence to pursuit of *real* justice…the justice of existence!

Chapter Nine

OBSTRUCTED "JUSTICE"

Distorted obedience

"Is it better to out-monster the monster or to be quietly devoured?"
~Friedrich Nietzsche

At this point, it should be much more apparent that a clear pattern of veiled and obstructed justice has been unleashed. The obstructions have come from duplicitous machinations of various "justice causes" and (in most cases) the strongholds from our own complicit mindset. This has produced a relative distorted obedience to charismatic personalities, political parties, and to justice movements and agencies, while preventing or obscuring allegiance to a committed stance for encouraging existence for all humankind.

By now, there should at least be an entry-level baseline capacity to discern what is truly right from that which is horribly wrong; and, what is innately "good" from things innately "evil." As more rigors are expended on dutiful introspection into the realm of the soul and spirit, sharper contrast and fine-tuning will be quickened, and further clarity and discernment will ensue. This should finally allow a standard of commitment to justly justice to emerge and take hold, and unity will finally characterize a real movement toward justice.

Popular 12-Step programs most frequently encourage participants to adhere to the mantra about "accepting the things I cannot change." This is a huge step for many, as "acceptance" can be a great transition and shift for bringing forth new life-changing realties and transformations for people stricken with debilitating habits and addictions. With a renewed commitment to justly justice however, a mantra that is quite similar but more conducive to our cause is, I am no longer accepting the things I cannot change, but changing the things I cannot accept. This essentially means that when it comes to the realm of "justice," there will not be tolerance for accepting the unacceptable; and, there will be a personal commitment to redouble efforts that ensure justly justice is the predominate motivation. In essence, a rigor to change things not acceptable!

The question that must be answered is, Going forward, what are some of the things that will no longer be acceptable? Will it be acceptable to endure ploys of manipulation that compel people into believing things and investing their time and emotions in untruths? Will it be acceptable to support unjust causes, people and personalities as long as they are of our favored political party and our favored political party "wins"? Will it be acceptable to reject justly justice and cower to peer pressures to help others (friends, family, co-workers, etc.) feel more comfortable? Irrespective of how passionate we are and how we think we may answer these questions, the bottom line is that we wont know how we will react until we are faced with having to deal with actual scenarios. Opportunities to stand for justice will continue to be ever-present and they will immediately challenge us and whether indeed we possess a true commitment to the standard of justly justice.

As a warm-up to the myriad issues that will need to be dutifully weighed and considered as they relate to real justly justice, an analysis of some of the more controversial issues will now be summarized and overviewed:

"CARING FOR THE POOR"

Rhetorical questions for consideration: Who are the poor? How do we best care for the poor? What is our sincere commitment to the poor? Is our commitment to the poor based on personal agenda and ideology, or is it based on facts, truth, justice, and/or commitment to Biblical writ? Will we reject any/all whom we may have supported and endorsed (prior) if we find they reject fundamental tenets of caring for the poor? Is it at all possible to claim fervent commitment to helping the poor, while rejecting its definition and fundamental tenets?

Current state: If we look at "the poor" in traditional terms, the U.S. is the most charitable nation in the world and actually does a good job of caring for its poor. Numerous charities and countless governmental aid programs provide a veritable "safety net" that prevents many from falling beneath base levels needed to survive and having to endure extreme hardship like what's commonly found in third-world countries. A safety net is deemed altruistic and most humane, but some have made what was supposed to be temporary help into a lifestyle of dependence; is this a good way to help/take care of our poor? Does encouraging and supporting programs for the poor that encourage a lifestyle of dependence goodly and Godly? With that said, it is clear more time should be spent clarifying and confirming a proper definition of "the poor" so we can proceed with unifying around how to finally solve this perpetual dilemma.

As noted throughout this book, if we are zealous about caring for the poor, we must first consider who would most appropriately fit this definition. Only then will we discern who are the poorest, most vulnerable, and most put-upon among us, and proceed to help. If we are objective and sincere, we would have to conclude the worst off and most vulnerable are those in the womb just wanting the opportunity to merely exist. If we portend we care for the poor, but don't have a committed stance in caring for the poorest among us by allowing them to just exist, we are lying to ourselves and have become the epitome of a hypocrite. If we laud and exalt people and/or agencies (by endorsing them, donating to them, voting for them, etc.), while they stand with old hatreds founded in eugenics to deny (or reject) the basic right to exist, it only confirms a strident commitment to political/party as a matter of 1st principle, not the poor! This definitively confirms the worst of willful self-deception, and the truth clearly belies purported commitment!

As ironic as it may sound, many (and especially "people of Faith") will still attempt to somehow rationalize their proclivities to support people or agencies who reject a base commitment to existence; they will surely attempt to use the Bible to further justify wretched dereliction on this issue. But the Bible provides no cover on this! In addition to the base commitment of upholding God's standards for bringing forth "life", throughout the entirety of the Bible" there are only four characterizations of what would classify as "the poor." These are: widows, orphans, the elderly, and the infirmed (handicapped). All others who have the capacity to work, but for some reason are *perpetually* non-working, are also classified but it is certainly not complimentary.

In the parable of the talents (Matt 25:14-30), it is confirmed that *everyone* has been given unique talents, skills and abilities! It is also confirmed that God expects everyone whom he has uniquely created to use these God-given abilities to His glory. Those who choose to bury, reject or underutilize God's unique yet perfect grace from ascribed skills and abilities are deemed as "wretched," "evil" and "unprofitable," and shall be condemned to "outer darkness." His exact pronouncement is, *"For to everyone who has will more be given (all the more), and he will be furnished richly so that he will have an abundance; but from the one who does not have (underutilized his talent and is therefore classified as "poor"), even what he does have will be taken away. And throw the good-for-nothing servant into the outer darkness; there will be weeping and grinding of teeth." (Matt 25:29-30 AMP).*

We can find another example of "the poor" by reviewing some of Apostle Paul's writings. In 2 Thessalonians 3, Paul outlines what is necessary to live a dignified life; he confirms and asserts personal responsibility through "work" is necessary. Essentially, he characterizes that if one doesn't work, he doesn't deserve to eat! Specifically, the text reads as follows: "... *with toil and struggle we worked night and day, that we might not be a burden or impose on any of you [for our support]. [It was] not because we do not have a right [to such support], but [we wished] to make ourselves an example for you to follow. For while we were yet with you, we gave you this rule and charge: If anyone will not work, neither let him eat. Indeed, we hear that some among you are disorderly [that they are passing their lives in idleness, neglectful of duty], being busy with other people's affairs instead of their own and doing no work."~ 2Thess 3:8-11.*

Finally, in 1 Timothy 5 it is clear that dereliction around providing support to people who really do not want to use their God-given skills, talents and abilities actually makes them worse than the worst evildoers! Specifically the text reads, *"Charge [the people] thus, so that they may be without reproach and blameless. If anyone fails to provide for his relatives, and especially for those of his own family, he has disowned the faith [by failing to accompany it with fruits] and is worse than an unbeliever.~* 1Tim 5:7-8. Is this what we want? Do we want to be complicit in producing segments of society and entire generations of people who should be "cast to outer darkness," and are worse than the worst evildoers? If not, our only response to the poor is to encourage their work and thriftiness and the building of their personal dignity through work!

By all notable and objective criteria, we have completely failed our "poor." We've miserably failed the unborn. We have failed those who choose to depend on government (by providing even more support for them to do so). And, we have failed to help the perpetually unemployed by failing to encourage ethics of hard work, entrepreneurship and diligence; instead, we have made it far too easy to be lethargic about skills, talents and abilities in each of us to be used for God's glory.

Justly justice grade: F. We have horribly failed here!

* * * *

Rhetorical questions for consideration: Is it possible to firmly commit oneself to all fundamental tenets of God's Word and also be liberal/progressive? Is the liberal/progressive mindset inherently "good" or "evil"? Is "liberation theology"/Black liberation theology wholly consistent with God's Holy writ? Based on what's been uncovered about justly justice, is there any logical explanation or Godly justification that is wholly consistent with supporting liberal progressive mindsets, agencies or political parties?

Current state: As previously noted with schemes from Hitler and Margaret Sanger (Hitler professed to be a "Christian" while committing his heinous acts, and Sanger used the "Black church" to preach the "merits" of abortion over the pulpit), the church and its respective leadership are under constant attack by the enemy of our soul. He masquerades and veils his horrendous acts as "enlightened," "just," and "utopian," while completely undermining God's own plans for His Kingdom. Throughout history, churches have been deceived and unwittingly used for "evil" under the pretense of "good." To be sure, "liberation theology" is definitively one of the demonically inspired schemes.

First and foremost, liberation theology is another gospel, and directly competes with the Gospel truth provided in the Holy Bible. The Apostle Paul in his rebukes and admonitions to churches of Galatia and Thessalonica, and in letters to Timothy, warns of deceptions that occur with people being seduced by other gospels, as opposed to strict adherence to the Gospel of purity and truth. Galatians 1:6-9 reads, "*I am astonished that you are so quickly deserting the one who called you to live in the grace of Christ and are turning to a different gospel— which is really no gospel at all. Evidently some people are throwing you into confusion and are trying to pervert the gospel of Christ. But even if we or an angel from heaven should preach a gospel other than the one we preached to you, let them be under God's curse! As we have already said, so now I say again: If anybody is preaching to you a gospel other than what you accepted, let them be under God's curse!"*~ NIV

It should now be clearer that liberation theology (in any form) is completely antithetical and must be considered a progressive evil! It has emanated from the exact same root of Communism embraced and enthroned by masters of evil like Hitler, Stalin, Mao, Lenin, Marx and many, many others. Since all these men were manifestly demonic, there is no redeeming "good" that can come from such a debased mindset and progressive liberal theology. Many have been used as tools of evil to pursue and convey liberality filled with purposely vague interpretations so as to confuse minds so people cannot discern the truth; this is especially notable with the brazen attack on *"the woman and her offspring."*

It should be noted that pro-abortion and committed racist stances are concentrated and infused throughout the liberation movement and related theology. There are many "pastors"/ministers/priests and Christians (in general) who are wholly complicit and unrepentant with this theology as it eviscerates God's creation, culminating with utter destruction of the unborn. There are many people who are seemingly smitten with embracing and enshrining political parties and politicians even while they (politicians) brag about being pro-abortion! They are equally enthused with the racial supremacy bias within these liberal progressive movements. How is this so? How can so many committed Christians willingly participate in the battle against God and His creation while supposedly fighting for God and His creation?

Deception reigns in the liberal progressive mindset. This mindset is notably evil, as it lives on lies because it comes from the father of lies (Satan). Justly justice and liberal progressive mindsets and theology are mutually exclusive. Due to its inherent damage to the Holy writ of the Bible and its deceptions that pervade and delude entire communities, it is impossible for someone to be committed to justly justice and also be committed to upholding and supporting liberal progressives or their debased mindsets! Liberalism and liberal progressives (in general) are a complete anathema to Christendom!

Justly justice grade: F. We've failed here!

* * * *

"WAR ON WOMEN"

Rhetorical questions to consider: If people stand and battle for *"the woman and her offspring"*, are they precipitating a "war *on* women" or a war *for* women? Can there be a "war on women" if people stand for policies that actually help women? If people stand in complete agreement with the women's right pioneer (Susan B Anthony) and the civil rights pioneer (Frederick Douglass) is it reasonable to say they are waging a "war on women"? If someone firmly opposes schemes and devices of slave owners, genocidal maniacs, and of racist/bigots of the past, to uphold and affirm "womanhood", are their actions a "war on women"? If perceptions about the "war on women" (abortions) are built on racial hatred, can it be legitimately deemed a "war on women", or should it be viewed as a scheme designed to proliferate a racist scourge?

Current state: Liberal progressive Supreme Court Justice, Ruth Bader Ginsberg, says she always thought abortion was not about women's rights, rather she knew "there was concern about population growth, and particularly growth in populations that we don't want to have too many of" (read Blacks/Hispanics). Shouldn't we take our Supreme Court Justice at her own word? We have confirmed through historical fact, racist miscreants like Margret Sanger strategically deployed abortion to eliminate "undesirables." The woman's rights pioneer, Susan B. Anthony, rejected abortion and worked diligently to eliminate it because of the many harms it causes for woman's health. As a product of rape (his mother was raped by a White slave master) the honorable Frederick Douglass teamed with Susan B. Anthony to help mitigate abortions. He also correctly noted that if exceptions were made for rape and/or incest, he and many thousands of others would not have had the opportunity to exist. This is the crux of the issue!

Life is proven to begin at conception, the unborn baby feels pain, and real justice is simply defined as the commitment to allow another to merely exist. Women are not served by rejecting facts, logic and reason about "life"; they can actually greatly harm themselves by embracing lies about abortion.

We should listen to the abortionist's own words when they say, "An abortion kills the life of a baby after it has begun." It is *dangerous to your life and health.* ...It may make you sterile, so that when you want a child you cannot have it..."(Planned Parenthood) . It is truly ironic and distorted that, people who want to prevent harmful effects that occur from abortion (physically and emotionally) are somehow castigated as waging a "war on women." Meanwhile, people who actually actively fight against "*the woman and her offspring*" by encouraging abortions, are somehow deemed enlightened and just as they verifiably fight and battle (God and His divine creation) on the side of evil!

The "war on women" mantra has been used to enshrine diabolical deeds of infanticide (around the world), Black Genocide and gender-cide (gender-specific abortion). It is a fact that many families in the U.S. are now casually deciding to end pregnancies because of the gender of the child; while its hard to imagine, gender-based/sex selection abortions are even more offensive and far worse than the already "generic-based" abortions. This is barbaric and most people would likely think this practice only happens in third-world countries. Regrettably, it is happening here in the U.S. and has been encouraged in and through acts of the U.S. congress! This is a real war being waged on women because the life of unborn females are (disproportionally) being denied the basic right to existence. When faced with the reality that many U.S. citizens are cavalierly making decisions to end the life of the unborn because of the impending gender of the child, the U.S. congress took up the issue. After legislation was written and brought to the floor to be voted on (Prenatal Nondiscrimination Act/PRENDA 2012), there were too many liberal progressive Democrats voting against ending this evil, so this barbaric and manifestly inhumane practice failed to pass! It was liberal progressive stalwarts and self-professed advocates for "justice" who voted to kill this bill (therefore, disproportionally, killing innocent baby girls), this abhorrent practice continues even to this day! We need to ask ourselves, Why didn't we hear about this notably evil practice and the Liberal progressives as they voted to uphold it? One-hundred sixty-eight people in congress voted to extend the practice that casually kills unborn females (mostly)! Again, by definition, this is the real war on women!! If we allow liberal progressive Democrat types to continue to rant about a purported "war on women" with impunity (no accountability to the facts surrounding this issue), we only further empower the evil subsidies of the battle being waged in the cosmic war between good and evil. Will we continue to empower them and their brazen and quite cynical rhetoric about women? Or, will we finally confront them and demand that they end their assaults against "the woman and her offspring"? For justly justice to take root and prevail, we must take a definitive stand for righteousness on this issue!

Justly justice grade: F-. We've horribly failed here!

* * * *

SOCIAL/RACIAL JUSTICE AGENCIES

Rhetorical questions to consider: Can agencies who define themselves as advocates for social and racial justice be taken seriously if they stand complicit with evil schemes to reduce or eliminate Blacks/Hispanics? Is it possible to sincerely advocate for a group or segment you actually help eliminate? Is fairness really a standard for justice, or does it actually empower evil? Can liberal progressives hold to any commitment to justice without regard for ensuring justice for the least and most vulnerable among us? Can any claims of racial injustices be taken seriously if the agencies that claim it fully embrace aborting the very communities they purport to protect?

Current state: This entire book has presented a preponderance of information and facts about real justice, and how current social justice movements and agencies are hypocrites at best and downright frauds at worst. Based on their own respective definitions, social/racial justices begin in the womb! To be sure, if agencies were truly committed to justly justice (justice that affirms the right to exist for the least and most vulnerable among us) the Southern Poverty Law Center (SPLC), ACLU, Congressional Black Caucus (CBC), NAACP, and LaRaza would all unite to ensure the evil racist bigoted machinations of liberal progressives will end. Because of the serious disproportional effects on "communities of color,"they would immediately renounce their support for Planned Parenthood and they would become stridently pro-life. They would gain a tremendous amount of adoration and respect for doing so, especially since an overwhelming majority of their key constituents (Blacks and Hispanics) are invariably pro-life and pro-family!

For far too long, people have hid behind ideology, political parties and personal leadership/fame to postulate and perpetuate nefarious deeds of evil masterminds. As we've noted, ill-defined terms like fairness have been the rule and guide for injustices, but it has horribly betrayed all of us. Earlier I alluded to "fairness" (in the context of equal outcome) as being demonic. This is an irrefutable fact! Fairness is the exact justification used in "eternity past" as the chief reason to rebel against God. Think about it, what was lucifer's justification for rebelling? Before he went on a rant of "I wills", lucifer stood chagrined with God because he didn't think it was "fair" that the Most High God had His divine nature and Kingdom. He rebelled because he coveted, he was jealous and, most importantly, he felt it wasn't "fair"! Hmmm, when we look at patterns of human behaviors and rants about fairness today, aren't they characterized by moods of covetousness and jealousies about what someone else has? If we are honest with ourselves, we will see the unmistakable connection between nebulous distinctions portending fairness and Lucifer's evil itself! The fact is, even if it were achievable, neither fairness in prosperity nor fairness in sheer misery would adequately suffice society's insatiable quest for the ever-elusive principle of fairness. Fairness has brought us this far in human history, and now its evils are notably unsustainable and indeed manifest. We must now reject this term altogether and really embrace the root of our social/racial justice issues...."justice"! Justice meaning the embracement of *existence*. Simply allowing others (all of humanity) to exist side-by-side with us is the epitome of justly justice!

Unfortunately, all existing "justice" movements have in some way helped result in an accepted cottage industry of death and destruction for the poorest and most needy among us. We have been captivated and complicit because we have unwittingly been duped into adopting the bondage of ideology, not principle. The only way to stop the current trajectory is to hold everyone purporting "justice" to an actual definitive criterion and a principle that upholds justice for all of humanity. Only the principle of justly justice will suffice as the acceptable standard going forward, and we will only succeed in stamping out hypocrisy and duplicity when we hold all (people, organizations, agencies, political parties, etc.) accountable to this righteous standard!

Justly justice grade: F. We have failed those who most need and deserve justice!

* * * *

OBAMACARE

Rhetorical questions to consider: If something is purportedly designed to help the poor, would it be designed to actually increase death and destruction to them? Can something be considered a good, just, and Godly cause if it actually undermines basic religious tenets and freedoms? Is it wise and prudent for leadership of churches/synagogues/parishes to wholly support policies that actually force them to participate in antithetical doctrine that is clearly antagonistic to their Faith?

Current state: At the outset, we should know and fully understand President Obama has been unkind to the unborn, and his namesake healthcare policies are wholly indicative of it. Contrary to Obama's many promises made to Catholic bishops, pastors and Faith organizations prior to its passage, according to official government estimates, Obamacare will dutifully prompt over 112,000 deaths of the unborn (via abortions) each year. Notwithstanding gross intellectual dishonesty, this should come as no surprise as, if nothing else, Obama has proven to be quite "expedient." When juxtaposing Obama rhetoric of "if we can just save one child…" with the realities of his policies, there is an unmistakable disconnect. Overseeing deaths of over 100,000 of the most innocent, however, is just the tip of the veritable iceberg for Obama and his Administration.

There is a quite troubling pattern of aggression toward the poorest and most innocent with our current president. One of the first actions he took when becoming president (in 2009) was to rescind the Mexico City Policy. This policy prevented all foreign countries/NGOs that receive U.S. government aid, from performing or promoting abortion services as a method of family planning; it is noteworthy, Clinton also rescinded it while he was president (both Bushes strictly enforced it). With this action, the U.S has again begun paying other countries over $500 million in aid each year as long as they proliferate abortions in their respective countries! Instead of helping end the scourge of abortion as it ravages the poorest within the poorest and most needy countries, the U.S. now again encourages and perpetuates it. Ironically, the justification for proliferating abortions to other countries is the same justification Margaret Sanger and others used. They contend that it is "humanitarian" and "compassionate" to eliminate the unborn, as we shouldn't want more people to be born into poverty stricken third-world countries; therefore, we should help them with population controls like abortion and sterilizations. While the cosmic battle between good/God and evil rages, we must still heartily contend with the elitist eugenics-based mindsets, as they are still having a huge impact on all of humanity!

It should be noted that Obamacare has far too many lies, failures and misdeeds to count. The most egregious is its demand for strict obedience to government! This tactic of providing "universal healthcare" in order to consolidate control and demand obedience to government is not new; both Hitler and Stalin trumpeted "universal healthcare" as a form of utopia to the masses. Under their administrations, government also demanded strict obedience to this government-run apparatus as it rendered another form of regressive enslavement for its respective citizenry. Utopian plans of providing universal healthcare never subsided; even after these failed regimes, most European nations held steadfastly to these ideals because its relative "predictability" was utilitarian and aided in ushering in universal miseries of planned economies. Like with all socialized schemes before it, Obamacare continues to demand that all bow to an all-powerful and ubiquitous government apparatus. It requires complete obedience as all healthcare providers bow to government, it demands doctors bow to government, and it demands all people in America bow to the iron-fisted demands of government (not to God and their respective Faith).

For many, Obamacare produced a whirlwind of transformations; it was these very transformations that obscured many of the nefarious objectives, so the actual demand for obedience in bowing to government was subtle and mostly unnoticed. The fact is, however, that Obamacare has allowed government to demand strict obedience in lieu of our Holy writ and Faith commitment to God. A good example is that doctors are now compelled (irrespective of their Faith/commitment to God) to provide abortive services to patients. There is no longer a conscience clause to protect doctors, nurses or any other service providers from being under the mandates of government! Further, hospitals (like some Catholic hospitals) are now mandated and must comply with new demands of government that require abortions/abortive services even though these types of services are antithetical to their founding and Faith foundations! Employers can no longer exercise their Faith/commitment, and are also dutifully mandated to bow to government by providing abortive services as part of "healthcare" to all employees!

Regrettably, a clear pattern that disrespects the unborn is manifestly clear with our president and his entire admiration. The Bible's admonishment that, "we shall know them by their fruit," should be especially poignant at this point. Please take a moment to consider, What is the Obama fruit? Our failure to hold him and our government (overall) to a standard of justly justice has cost many millions of lives around the world, and this scourge will surely continue unless we learn to unify and act consistently to battle against it, and for God!

Justly justice grade: F-. Obamacare is an abject failure at providing justice!

* * * *

IMMIGRATION REFORM

Rhetorical questions to consider: If political parties and respective agencies look at "immigration" as a way to expand voting bloc and/or gain influence, are they actually compassionate? If we condone maiming and killing of human beings just looking for a better life, is that compassionate? If immigrants are fundamentally being looked upon and preyed upon/manipulated as a "voting bloc" and political "pawns," instead of as fellow human beings, can we assert compassionate motivations? Is it wise, prudent and just for any country to encourage "open borders" and mass immigration while allowing the vilest of evil to proliferate on its borders (via terrorists/threats, and human/drug traffickers)? What is the most compassionate and justly justice method to handle immigration reform(s)?

Current state: The best way to address this contentious issue is to see it through a realistic metaphor. Metaphorically consider the following scenario: As a homeowner, you decide to take steps to put a swimming pool in your backyard. You proceed with all proper channels including engineering and design, and finally get to the building/permit stage. As a final condition of the permit for the swimming pool, the city/county office confirms that as a condition of the permit, you must have fencing around the pool. You proceed with the pool and once completed enjoy its use! Then, on one Friday night before leaving town, you and your entire family enjoy the pool, but because of the inconvenience of it all, you decide to leave the pool unsecured (no fencing). While you are away on the weekend getaway, the neighbor and his son decide to sneak a swim, and (regrettably you discover upon your return) they have both drowned. What will be the response from surrounding neighbors? How will law enforcement respond? The easy answer is, you will be viewed as having precipitated in taking the life of the neighbor and his son, and you will be immediately taken to jail in handcuffs by law enforcement! You will be charged with two deaths because you knew what the law/permit required, yet you were negligent and your negligence served as an inducement to the neighbors (and the subsequent loss of life). Now, this is *exactly* analogous to what we see with our border issues! Does LaRaza protest that our open borders are an inducement to death and destruction of the people they are purportedly committed to protect? Are liberal progressives outraged by the amount of sheer death, destruction and untold and unmentionable accounts of raped women and girls have to endure as a result of our inducement? Does the various women's organizations protest about the abuse of women/girls and the horrors many of them have to endure just to get to the U.S? Do they say anything about the preponderance of human trafficking and forced servitude/prostitution women and girls are susceptible to as a result of our porous borders? Irrespective of unmentionable human suffering (e.g., rape, molestation, assault, and death) is LaRaza and other agencies complicit in encouraging illegal human trafficking just to further their political aspirations through "sacrificial lambs" and "by any means necessary"? Can this, in any way, be construed as justice? Caesar Chavez had it right on this issue! Because of the impending disaster and human toll open borders/illegal immigration posed on the U.S. labor force, and because of the impending personal tragedies women and children looking to cross the border would be susceptible to, Caesar Chavez stood ardently against any illegal trekking from Mexico to the U.S.; he was principled on this issue! Do we have *any* principled "leaders" or agencies who will stand to decry this human rights tragedy and scourge today?

Lets consider another analogy that should help us confirm the need for border protections. Let's say you have neighbors who (for some reason) hate you to the extent they utterly despise even looking at you. Let's say they have announced they want to kill you and your entire family, and are constantly threatening your very existence. If this were the case, would it at all make sense for you leave your front door wide open? Would you leave all your doors and windows unlocked even at night and even when you are away? Would you leave your entire backyard unfenced and unprotected? Knowing evil people are intent on killing you and your family, would you allow your entire family (including children) to frolic up and down the street without so much as a wary eye or protection?

This is exactly what we face with evil cowardice terrorists/groups who are hell-bent (literally) on killing Americans and our way of life! Several years ago the U.S. government confirmed Al Qaeda is actively using our southern borders to penetrate deep indie the U.S. It was also proven other terrorist agencies are actively using our porous borders. Does this make sense at all? At this time on our history, does it seem prudent for our president and his minions in congress to desire less border enforcement? Is it acceptable for the U.S., with its many enemies, to usurp laws requiring added security in order to ensure there is less protections and open borders that induce acts of evil cowardice?

The fact is, taking up the immigration issue without a precondition of a secure border, is nonsensical! It cannot be defended from the standpoint of helping people looking for a better life (as many are killed or maligned), nor can it be defended from the standpoint of not needing additional security fencing to protect against terrorist/organizations. Wisdom and prudence to protect lives in both cases would demand immediate additional border security/fencing. Then and only then can we begin to determine how to best handle immigration going forward.

Too many people have been permanently maimed, psychologically damaged or killed as a result of our disastrous polices on the border, and both political parties are at fault! Actually, none of us can escape blame on this issue because whether you support it or not, we all now have blood on our hands. In true contrition and sorrow, we all should weep for the hundreds of thousands of people who have been horribly killed (or have been maligned in some manner) with hopes to find and secure a better life. In a tragic irony, our current Obama Administration's Department of Justice hatched and precipitated one of the most notoriously evil acts that even to this day continues to plague our borders with untold death and destruction. President Obama and his U.S. Department of Justice Chief (Eric Holder) concocted a scheme to put over 2000 high-powered assault rifles into hands of Mexican drug and human traffickers! To this day, there is no logical explanation as to why they supported this horribly flawed and seemingly mindless policy. According to reports, every year since their gross dereliction, over 10,000+ people have been maimed or killed on or near the U.S/Mexico borders. There have been numerous deaths and destruction traced back to the very assault rifles the DOJ provided to Mexican drug and human trafficking kingpins.

There have also been U.S border patrol agents maimed and killed by our DOJ-supplied assault rifles! Most regrettably, no one has been held accountable! Can this be considered justice in any way, shape or form? Is our border policies humanitarian and compassionate at all? Does it make sense to encourage, induce and manipulate unsuspecting people (just looking for a better life) to put their lives and the life of their family in danger? Because of its ability to prevent great tragedies, is securing the U.S./Mexico border wise and "good" for all humanity, or is it "evil"?

In the end, we can see all policies regarding illegal immigration must include increased preemptive security/fencing in order to protect lives; this will protect U.S. citizens lives, and the lives of people currently being induced and indoctrinated into subjecting themselves to incredible risks by trekking across the U.S. border. This is logical and is the only logical and compassionate stance toward a *real* justice! **Justly justice grade: F- Blood is poring off our hands as we have failed all humanity with these incoherent immigration schemes and polices!**

* * * *

Rhetorical questions to consider: Should all people make approximately the same income? Should a highly trained doctor/surgeon really make the approximate equivalent of a mechanic or bus driver? If the official government agency (CBO) says raising the minimum wage will certainly eliminate 500,000-1,000,000 jobs, is it still worthy of supporting? Would income equality still provide people impetus for higher education (pursuit of higher Education/degrees) and work incentives (employment mobility)? If all people made relatively equivalent incomes, would there be any incentive toward upward mobility? Do societies progress if there is no incentive for personal improvement? Would innovations and entrepreneurship still be viable if all incomes were relatively the same, or would people opt to just remain in minimalist jobs of rote? Did God put individual skills, talents and abilities in each person so He would get glory out of our personal pursuits? If God gave us unique abilities, doesn't it tacitly confirm He rejects the notion of "sameness"?

Current state: Income inequality has always been a part o the human experience! Even in Biblical times income/wealth inequality has been tacitly ordained. When children of Israel escaped Egypt and spent 40 years in the wilderness, Biblical record confirms there were landowners, there were Levitical priests and there were indentured bondservants/slaves; all these groups had different roles, duties, income, and wealth dynamics! God dutifully ordained it all! So, is God anti-equality? In the sense of outcome-based equality, the answer is definitively yes!

As mentioned prior, God abhors "sameness" or "fairness" in the sense of outcomes; He didn't create robots, He created people as unique instruments of His divine nature and manifest glory. Further, He wants unique glory coming from every aspect of His creation! God is the ultimate arbiter of justice, and He sees justice as each person having equal opportunities to accomplish what He created them to do, but it never connotes equal outcomes. We should know, any demand for equal outcomes denotes covetousness and jealousy while fundamentally usurping God's divine authority as our source. Demand for equal outcomes forces men to put all their trust in men (government/institutions) as the primary arbiter of "justice," while rejecting God's authority and plans. This is notably evil and antithetical!

A rejection of God as our only and ultimate source is demonic, and was posited in the human psyche from atheistic minds like Plato, Thomas More, Thomas Hobbes, and Karl Marx. All these men had one fundamental thing in common, a commitment to reject the notion of God; because of their commitment to atheism and hatred and rejection of God, they sought to replace the unseen "God notion" with something that can be seen, government! This again is the mindset that permeated the worst genocidal maniacs of all human history. All nefarious dictators in human history trumpeted "income inequality" as justification for usurping the will of the people, while consolidating governmental powers unto themselves. Most notably, all these notorious miscreants completely failed on all promises for prosperous equality! However, they did accomplish equality in the form of shared misery. When a society runs out of other people's money, hard work, innovation, and entrepreneurship, shared misery is a certainty! Is this the kind of justice we yearn for? Do we want a Godly plan that aligns with maximizing unique skills, talents and abilities, or are we just looking for governmental schemes to manipulate us into believing impossible utopian dreams of atheists?

When it comes to income inequality, we should cherish and trust the motivations and inspirations that come from each individual. This is God's creation working as He intended! It is good to have a workforce that is designed to allow young people to enter the workforce as teenagers and, based on their own rigor and tenacity, ascend to higher levels of income as they grow older and take additional responsibility. Even with our horrible economy wrought with malaise, this still happens! If someone gets an entry-level job, there is incentive to learn the skill and look to get promotion to the next level as mastery occurs. After a certain level of mastery, it is reasonable to look to ether get a promotion, or pursue additional education to permit a transition to another employ that will provide even more opportunity for growth and personal expansion. This cycle continues until people are satisfied that they have reached their personal pinnacle or are content.

If we somehow mandate income equality (or significantly increase the minimum wage) through government fiat, the entire cycle changes. Employers who normally provide entry-level jobs to teenagers/minors, would quite obviously look to more seasoned adults to fill those positions (because of the increased wage scale). They would also likely incorporate a strictly part-time workforce (due to Obamacare mandates, and mandated wage scale). Further, many will have to dramatically increase their prices of goods/service (because new wage scale puts undue pressure on profits), but most small/medium-sized businesses will be forced to permanently close their doors! In the end, this will greatly increase unemployment and further spread undue misery and pain throughout communities. Most of the people hurt or affected will be younger, lower skilled and less educated people. Most notably, government-mandated income equality measures/policies would certainly disproportionally harm "communities of color" as prices for food and necessities will have to "necessarily skyrocket"! Is this really what we want? Can this be construed as justly justice in any way shape or form?

As further confirmation, a study by the University of California, Irvine in 2007 assessed studies for the last two decades about the impact of a minimum wage increase on employment. "A sizable majority of the studies surveyed in this monograph give a relatively consistent (although not always statistically significant) indication of the negative employment effects of minimum wages. In addition, among the papers we view as providing the most credible evidence, almost all point to negative employment effects, both for the United States as well as for many other countries," the UC Irvine study stated. The facts about this issue are manifest! Applying our own wisdom, knowledge and prudence to this issue will allow us to see more clearly without the over simplification of hyperbolic rhetoric coming from our president and the minions in the media who (as a matter of 1st principle) are wholly committed to transforming America by any means necessary!

In the end, income inequality has been around since the beginning of mankind; it is established and ordained! God has unique abilities He put in each of us, and He wants to receive glory from each of us. Mandated income equality measures detract our focus from our true source (God), while empowering the insidious and diabolical (government) to undermine our innate calling. Our incentive to learn, grow and progress comes from innate structures existing within a dynamic workforce built upon concepts of entrepreneurial mobility!

To help finalize and confirm thoughts about income inequality, we should consider wisdom from the great Thomas Sowell. In a recent article, Sowell writes of "The Blessings of Inequality" (by Rick Pearcey, January 28, 2014): "We are lucky that we are so different, so that the capabilities of many other people can cover our limitations. But more than this, the inequality of abilities (or "diversity," one might say) we see in human beings can save lives and enhance 'everyone's well-being.' Yes, human beings are created equal, as the Declaration of Independence so appropriately notes. This fact of life affirms the ontological worth and significance of the human being. It expresses the basis upon which people are to be respected by the powers that be and not steamrolled by big government, big business, big media, big 'ministry,' big Hollywood, big 'science,' or big anything. Thus government, business, ministry, and so on, are created to serve man. Man is not created to worship and serve any of these entities. But note: Human beings are created equal *in their individuality*, as well. All of us have fingerprints, and yet every set of fingerprints is unique. In the human being, therefore, both unity and diversity are equally affirmed. When diversity -- or inequality, properly understood -- is respected, our lives are enriched (in creativity, achievement, healing, wealth, and so on). *Vive la différence.* The opposite is equally true. When diversity (or inequality) is disrespected, our lives are impoverished. Freedom, ideas, speech, excellence, and creativity begin to disappear as society is herded down the road to serfdom, to borrow a phrase. Diversity can also be deified. But this is a bad move because, as an idol, diversity breeds chaos -- even if it is well marketed (diversity is our strength). Chaos in morals and politics is, of course, unlivable. And so the temptation comes: Let us organize our lives around 'unity.' But when unity is grasped as a final solution, when it is deified in reaction to the totalizing god of 'diversity,' the real-world result is uniformity and oppression. The individual is smashed in the name of equality (or 'fairness,' 'tolerance,' etc.). All too quickly, a people faces an elitist steamroller of presidential pens and phones, of federal laws and regulations, of dog-whistle peer pressure seeking to impose pretended absolutes enforced by those who hold power at a particular moment in history. How do we move forward to achieve individual and corporate balance? By realizing that both unity and diversity are gifts from the Creator. They are too wondrous and powerful to be left in the hands of politicians."

When it's all said and done, can income inequality be considered a just cause? Are we going to be complicit with the serendipitous manipulations from government to seize liberty and freedoms based in the need for income inequality? Will we allow God to get maximum glory out of our individual pursuits? This issue is now ours to further contemplate either wholly accepting or Holy rejecting!

Justly justice grade: This is still to be determined; if government mandates new wage scales/minimum wage standards for all businesses, we will have failed!

It is notable that while each of the aforementioned populist themes have been promoted as issues that confirm some form of intolerance or injustice, in actuality they prevent and obstruct justice. Heretofore, we have lacked depth and perspective and this is what has skewed our perspective. Now we should be able to more clearly view each of these issues in proper context and with appropriate balance and perspective.

In summary of this chapter, we should now be able to appropriately discern that some of our impediments to receiving truth have been due to strongholds residing in either the soul or spirit. We have attempted to nourish and appropriately intervene in these areas by increasing the capacity to observe them in order to produce a tangible shift. At the very least, we were able to uncover truth and a depth of additional perspective surrounding the most pressing issues of our day. In the end, we see that most of our thoughts and ideas about these issues needed more grounding and understanding from additional points of view. There is no delusion that many will still attempt to fight the facts, dismiss the truth and reject evidences presented. Now, however, we know that these people are enslaved to their own derelictions and harness well-entrenched moods that have been infused with propaganda from masterminds that in many ways cripple and prevent them from moving forward and encouraging the development and well-being of all mankind. These people are stricken to produce moods that are racist, self-serving and duplicitous, and therefore are precluded from living the good life full of grace as God intended! If people and agencies come to know and accept the truth about justly justice, they will see how to move from relative brokenness represented as crags of jagged and debased ideology, to the true fullness represented by riches and full glory.

Chapter Ten

FROM CRAGS TO RICHES

Goodness is the only investment which never fails.

~ Henry David Thoreau

All justice movements want and need to be successful. Justice, real justice, helps all humankind! The key to success going forward is to move from relative crags (representing broken and jagged edges of debased ideology) to riches via industry-wide embodiment and holistic understanding of justice as encompassing mankind's "basic" universal right to exist.

If we as a nation and society are to succeed in helping encourage real justice, we should only dutifully support agencies and people who are firmly committed to real justly justice! Agencies will be able to move from merely existing to resoundingly flourishing if they finally come to the realization and acknowledgment that all injustice is injustice, and therefore as a matter of 1st principle they must necessarily encourage the right to merely exist as a universal right for all mankind. I believe many involved in the justice movement have unnecessarily floundered due to incoherent and hypocritical stances. A new/renewed commitment to real justice will provide a holistic, irreproachable and perfectly congruent approach to justice; it will also greatly increase workers and donations from a new and reinvigorated donor base! People will readily invest time, skills, resources, etc. if they perceive consistency without contrived hypocrisy.

Hypocrisy is the number-one enemy to justice. It has been well documented that labels like social justice, racial justice and human rights can easily be used to gin momentum in producing a range of emotions and immediate actions, without even making a dent in curing injustices. To be sure, emotions like anger and outrage are often used to increase donations and solicit fervent endorsements/support, but little else. Since donors and advocates fund and perpetuate advancement of the various people and agencies purporting a "justice" cause, shouldn't we hold them accountable for delivering quantifiable results? What happens if all these agencies are now held accountable for real justice that begins in the womb? If indeed the various agencies (and leadership/personalities thereof) continue to postulate justice in primarily political terms with a focus on political ends and no definitive commitment to "life," all donations should cease. We will confirm they have no real conviction for justly justice and are just looking to operate with impunity while taking full advantage of our good graces.

It would be presumptive to assert the entire cottage industry of "justice" agencies are so calculating and cynical about their cause that they only seek to use their respective members and advocates to gain maximum social/political clout. On the other hand, it would also be rather unwise to discount this possibility! As a matter of 1st principle, many of these agencies look to gain politically through accolades and attribution from nefarious political masterminds, not from an altruistic approach to justice. There is no doubt that many well-intended purely altruistic people have been a part of these respective agencies as great workers and friends of the causes. Like me, they have invested their time and treasures to trumpet injustices, and they are now chagrined to see that so little has been accomplished. Our actions going forward will dictate the trajectory of justice movements. If we withhold all funding until respective justice agencies validate their commitment to human existence, we will see a great change toward real justly justice. However, if we continue to invest our time and treasures knowing these people and agencies are complicit with the horrors of slave masters, eugenics, Sanger, etc., we will continue to add to the approximately 60 million deaths of the most innocent!

The fact is, we now have the capacity to discern whether indeed justice agencies and advocates are sincerely and legitimately concerned about the poorest of the poor, the most needy and the innocents most incapable of speaking out for themselves. Based on the respective definitions used by the justice causes, this is the specific demographic to which these agencies are purportedly designed to cater. With our new definitions, we can now begin to appropriately hold them accountable to their own designated standards, and actually change the entire justice industry with a simple shift! It is clear that a shift toward allowing human existence as a matter of 1st principle would unify the justice movement, and appropriately deconstruct the otherwise complex issues of justice so it can now be "easily" accomplished. The time to fight for justly justice is now!

A consistent theme throughout this book has pointed to how, through our relative sensibilities, we have been manipulated and duped into supporting causes we thought were committed to help all mankind! Little did we know, most of these organizations and their respective leadership actually lack support for those who are truly poor and most innocent. Unless and until we demand accountably to the 1st principles of justly justice, our sensibilities and gullibility's will continue to be targeted and threatened by agencies and individuals who don't share the concept of "life" being a fundamental right. The urgency of justly justice demands an answer and our answer must be to forge relationships with real leaders committed to real justice. Doing so will enrich and reinvigorate the entire justice industry and prevent further scourge, assault and judgment on the American spirit! Again, if agencies adopt a new stance, a more principled stance, they will be richly rewarded. But they will not make any shift in stance unless we demand it and hold them accountable.

It should now be apparent that income inequality, racial inequality, environmental justice, marriage inequality, social justice, human rights, immigration rights, environmental justice, etc, are all meaningless unless and until we confirm a universal commitment to just giving the basic right to simply exist. It is now time to move toward specific solutions that help confirm necessary actions we can take to support the coming forth of all of humanity.

Chapter Eleven

POTENT POIGNANT PRINCIPLED

Solutions moving forward

The wicked flee when no man pursueth, but the righteous are bold as a lion.
~The Bible

An old axiom confirms that "all that is necessary for the triumph of evil is that good men do nothing." ~Edmund Burke This is the definitive truth about our plight going forward! Even with all the new facts and truths that have been uncovered about the real justice (justly justice), none of it will matter if it doesn't prompt us into immediate action. The simple fact is if we do nothing, injustices will continue to prevail and pervade all of humanity. Tens of millions more of the unborn will be denied their basic right to existence, as schemes targeted against humanity fester, coagulate and gain momentum in the epic battle between good and evil. With its designs against God and His divine creation, evil will accelerate unless we take definitive principled actions to slow its momentum and ultimately stop it!

During the 1800s, reverend William J.H. Boetcker wrote about relative malaise people exhibited during rather quite turbulent times in the middle to late 1800s; he famously wrote about seven national crimes: 1. I don't think. 2. I don't know. 3. I don't care. 4. I am too busy. 5. I leave well enough alone. 6. I have no time to read and find out. 7. I am not interested. Admittedly, these are the same national crimes that have allowed rampant injustices to prevail. Boetcher's seven national crimes have plagued us during times of slavery, during Susan B. Anthony's initiation of women's rights, during the expansion of eugenics, during Hitler's respective slaughter of millions of Jews, and certainly the crimes are plaguing us during these dark times of

Margaret Sanger's schemes precipitating Black genocide. The seven national crimes are a primary impediment that precludes transitioning us to a country wholly committed to justly justice! As with Boetcher's admonition, the pursuit of justice requires action.

After this reading, will we accept lethargy and indifference that further numbs our sensibilities, or will we become engrossed with the clear need for justice for the poorest and most innocent? Are we now better able to understand that labels and distinctions portending justice have blinded and betrayed us, therefore making necessary the rejection of all labels?

A recurring theme and key factor that has aided and abetted the "justice industry" is ungrounded labels connoting justice. People have labeled themselves "justice advocates." Organizations and agencies have labeled themselves "justice agencies." And politicians have labeled themselves "justice advocates." All of these labels have failed us! As noted, most of those participating in justice movements are ardently anti-life/pro-abortion, so they literally have no real sense or semblance of justice. As we see, all these labels are meaningless unless they are definitively committed to a basic precondition of simply allowing all humankind to merely exist!

Foremost among those who seek to gain maximum leverage from strategic yet insidious labeling are politicians, political parties and political movements. There are politicians want to assert they are committed to "justice" while remaining in the good graces of Planned Parenthood (as we've seen with Jesse Jackson, for instance). Political parties (like the Democrat Party, for instance) want to assert they are the only party standing for justice, while concurrently remaining in the graces of Planned Parenthood and fully funding their schemes of Black genocide (approximately $550 million in taxpayer funds) and scourge against the poorest and most innocent of all humanity. Justice agencies (like NAACP, CBC, LaRaza, SPLC, etc.) want to say they stridently stand for various justice causes, while concurrently supporting and endorsing candidates wholly committed to proliferating the worst scourge known to man! The point is, going forward we must resolve to resoundingly reject all labels and strictly look first to the principles of existence/"life" to guide our actions of support. Since it has been poignantly confirmed that all injustice *is* injustice, we should see and appreciate that these new criteria are the only way to help us finally institute a new baseline to build upon as we look to help eradication of all injustices afflicting humankind.

While labels can be useful, today's labels exhorting political parties/candidates and relative "justice" movements have been unscrupulously used to deceive us; through strong traditions and affiliations with Political Party identification, we have allowed them to become inextricably imbedded in the realm of our soul and spirit, and now they manifest themselves as unshakable heartstrings and soul-ties. Nefarious masterminds look to fully leverage the current hypersensitive label-conscious climate, as they purpose to grip and sweep us into an entrenched ideology and a mindset that demand blind allegiance to their perverted sense of justice. It is particularly troublesome that, through the act of casting our vote, we have unwittingly empowered unrelenting mindsets that grip our very soul and spirit; they overrule our committed life stance while supporting entities that undermine our beliefs. The fundamental transgression that allows an active undermining of our principles comes from our vote. To be sure, consider our current president. While most would not agree with his fervent desire to proliferate abortions-on-demand around the world, his lauding and applauding Margaret Sanger, and his ardent commitment to fund Planned Parenthood with federal taxpayer funds, he received overwhelming support from Black (97%+) and Hispanic (70%+) communities; ironically, these are the very communities which are disproportionally targeted via Sanger's racist schemes and are in the forefront of an epic battle for "*the woman and her offspring*"! Even with his less than stellar first-term track record, the collective voting patterns of these communities put Obama over the top for a second term. This makes it abundantly clear that we have power in our vote; each and every individual vote counts, and collectively our votes could actually empower evil, or move "mountains" toward good!

Imagine for a second what would happen if the Black community stood united against *all* schemes proliferating black genocide and proponents of Margaret Sanger's eugenics-based racism (i.e., today's liberal progressives like Justice Ginsberg, who says abortion is designed to eliminate those whom we do not want too many of)? Of course, this would mean we could no longer support Barack H. Obama, Hillary R. Clinton and most of the Democrat Party, but real justice will begin to prevail! The question is, could we actually end support of these individuals and their respective institutions? Are our "spirit-ties" so strong that we will continue to allow ourselves to be usurped by brazenly debased ideology? We cannot have it both ways! Either we have the fortitude and personal courage (like that of Frederick Douglass) to leave partisan party politics behind and just stand for justly justice, or we will continue to be willingly enslaved by evil ideology. At some point, we must eschew party labels and partisan party politics and just vote for whoever stands for the 1st principle of embracing all humankind's right to exist. If we have the courage to vote in accordance with our faith and personal convictions, we will truly be able to change America into a nation committed to real justly justice. But, make no mistake a discernable change in the arena of justice must start with how we vote!

What would happen if the women's right movement stood unified with the pioneer of the women's movement, Susan B. Anthony, and rejected Planned Parenthood's schemes that actually harm women? If Planned Parenthood were actually held accountable for its own words like, "an abortion kills the life of a baby after it has begun" and "it is *dangerous to your life and health,*" women should be able to universally rebuke and reject their diabolical schemes. Again, just casting votes for those committed to rejecting Planned Parenthood can change the trajectory of this agency and the plight of our country overnight. The question becomes, Does knowing more of the historical facts/truths about the foundations of the women's rights movement prompt immediate rejection and denouncement of Planned Parenthood? Will we now be able to change the conversation about women's rights to include that of the life of the most innocent? Again, women can't have it both ways! They can't assert to be a women's rights justice advocate and also be a pro-abort advocate; because of the real nature of "justice" these two stances are mutually exclusive.

What would happen if the Faith community (inclusive of pastors/priests/ministers/Parrish leaders/rabbi's, etc.) stood completely unified in an unbreakable bond to an unwavering commitment to uphold justly justice as a 1st principle? What would they be able to accomplish if they chose to no longer be used as tools fighting on behalf of secular humanists, atheists and all others battling on the side of evil while seeking to undermine and destroy Gods divine nature promulgated via life? What if they took a public stand and committed they shall not, they cannot and absolutely will not vote or support ***anyone*** who does not embrace existence/life as a 1st principle for all humankind? If this happens, America's voting patterns would immediately change, and God would be glorified!

The clarion call of life/existence is a uniting force that will help restore, revive and reunite God's people with His supreme authority and divine nature. The earth groans, awaiting for the manifestation of all mankind to join in the epic battle for real justice! God has been waiting "for such a time as this" for people of Faith to finally unite and fight in His cosmic battle against evil for *"the woman and her offspring."* The poignant reality is, this cosmic battle culminates with something precious we each have in our individual control-our vote!

If we care about true justice, we must care about politics and the act of voting! The vote is one of the most powerful and strategic tools empowering every American citizen. By the preponderance of us just taking the action to cast our vote we can immediately change America. It is what establishes and ensures real justice! In the book of Exodus, God commanded the Israelites to choose their representatives, but He also told them to make sure they were capable, God-fearing and trustworthy (Ex 18:2-23); we are to keep these characteristics and principles at the forefront (in perpetuity) as we choose those who lead this nation. Let's ask ourselves, based on our current White House and Congress, how have we done in this regard? Undoubtedly we failed! For some reason, people have rejected the need and responsibility to vote (as God commanded) and therefore are complicit tools for evil. Secular humanists, Marxist and others with nefarious goals have achieved immense power because their demented followers are quite zealous to vote, while (for the most part) people of Faith have been lethargic and therefore complicit. We (good/Godly) greatly outnumber them; therefore, it is cruel, irresponsible and grossly unjust for us not to perform the simple act of voting! If we unify around recognizing the significance of our vote, we will show we are indeed a force to be reckoned with for righteousness and the commitment to justice.

Voting in accordance with the 1st principles of real justice will finally allow us to achieve a justly just nation! If we come together and unify behind real justice while fully utilizing our vote, we will indeed be able to move mountains in America! With purposeful righteousness as our standard, we will be able to tear down mountains of transgressions and begin a new season of renewal and revival. For this to occur, we must have the intestinal fortitude to utterly reject people we may have unwittingly supported in the past. While there is no litmus test for justly justice, a litmus test can be used to help us adroitly clarify and confirm our vote. The test can be confirmed with a series of simple questions like, Does this person believe in the 1st principle of justly justice (allowing existence to just come forth)? Would women's right pioneer, Susan B. Anthony, vote for this person? Would the civil rights pioneer, the Honorable Frederick Douglass vote for this person? If He were still walking the earth, would Jesus (Himself) cast a vote for this person even as he/she battles against His Father's creation? Would the unborn vote for this person? Would God himself vote for this person and his/her respective policies? This series of questions provides all we need to pursue justly justice in our actions and our vote!

Voting is a primary tool that we must use to help assure a new beginning for real justice in America and around the world. With that in mind, there are some who have a long track record of standing opposed to real justly justice, and we must redouble the effort to end support and vote them out. To be sure, we must stand united in no longer supporting *any* state governors with debased mindsets like Jerry Brown (Governor of California), Martin O' Malley (Governor of Maryland), Andrew Cuomo (Governor of New York), just to name a few. It also means complete rejection of Senators like Chuck Schumer (NY), Dick Durbin (IL), Kirsten Gillibrand (NY), Al Franken (MN), Robert Menendez (NJ) Barbara Boxer (CA), and Dianne Feinstein (CA) again to name a few; based on their reprehensible track record, these people are a menace to "life" (and entire societies) as they ruthlessly reject extending life to poorest and most needy in humanity! Also, while there are again far too many to list, we will completely reject *any* support for some House Members including Keith Ellison (MN.), Barbara Lee (CA), James Clyburn (SC), Sheila Jackson Lee (TX), Donna Edwards (MD.), Mike Honda (CA), Maxine Waters (CA), Luis Gutiérrez (IL), Alcee Hastings (FL), Elijah Cummings (MD), and Linda Sanchez (CA), for starters. These are some of the worst offenders at encouraging the scourge of what Jesse Jackson appropriately deemed as "Black genocide"; they have no sensitivity to the plight of the most needy, and by default support the proliferation of the grossest of gross injustices against all mankind. To be sure, we do not have anything personal against these individuals; we do not dislike them or are "haters" of them. Our commitment to real justice, however, precludes us from any support, endorsement or votes for them! Because they are harbingers of manifest injustice, they must be immediately replaced! After replacing them with new State Governors, Senators, and House members, we will be able to demand that any new Supreme Court nominations must meet a minimum threshold of upholding justly justice as a 1st principle. And in 2016, a commitment to vote strictly for those who align with the principle of justly justice is an achievable the first step for unifying to vote for a new "justly just" president. "Yes we can." We can and we will indeed change America!

Another solution that we must adopt to ensure success in accomplishing justly justice requires that we strictly invest our time and treasures in real justice agencies. Instead of giving our time, sweat and treasures to agencies that may be well-meaning, but lack commitment to really helping the least among us (the unborn), we need to focus our attention on strictly providing resources to those committed to the 1st principle of justly justice. For instance, while the Red Cross, United Way, NPR, ACLU, etc., are organizations and agencies that we may have donated to in the past, we should now look to redirect finances to organizations committed to using donations to provide community impact in the quest toward ending injustice! Excellent agencies like the Frederick Douglass Foundation, Issues for Life Foundation, National Black pro-life Congress, Alveda King Ministries, Radiance Foundation and National Black pro-life Coalition are just a few organizations already committed to the 1st principle of justly justice! Support for these agencies and their respective leadership is worthwhile as they have been battling for real justice for many years and they need our support to ensure that we end the cycle of injustice as it specifically targets segments and communities for elimination.

In combination with our vote and our donations, another quite powerful solution that should be deployed to encourage justly justice is spreading of the truth via word of mouth. If we will commit to spreading the facts and truths about real justice to everybody we know, we can educate to the point that attitudes will begin to change. More importantly, if we can spread the word about justly justice by providing this book to all our friends, family, coworkers, community activists, "justice" advocates/agencies, and all elected officials, we can begin to permanently change the trajectory of America. Likewise, informing all leaders in churches, synagogues, and parishes about justly justice, and inviting them to engage in intensive workshops/trainings/forums on the issues covered within this book will also help spread the good news about justice while helping stave off injustice. We should certainly see more Godliness and less hypocrisy; we will also have far less liberal progressive lies and talking points spread via the pulpit. The bottom line is, providing this book to our entire network will help proliferate justly justice throughout America and around the world. Are you willing to commit to this cause? Will you commit to getting multiple copies for your friends? Will you get 10, 20, 30 or 50 copies to help proliferate this much-needed and timely truth?

There is much to do and we have far to go! Countless numbers of the unborn are mercilessly killed each and every day. Even with the ominous task ahead, we can certainly accomplish helping real justice to prevail. The Honorable Frederick Douglass once said, "one and God make a majority." This statement is quite true! As we yield ourselves (mind, body and resources) to God we are indeed the majority. With our firm commitment to winning the epic battle for good, God will get the glory!

Our vote, our donations/investment and our word-of mouth testimony are strategic tools to be deployed in Gods battleground. Are you ready to fight with and for Him? Let's go!

CONCLUSION

"Many who think themselves infinitely superior to the aberrations of Nazism, and sincerely hate all manifestations, work at the same time for ideals whose realization would lead straight to the abhorred tyranny."

–F.A. Hayek

Throughout this book, we confirmed that we have arrived at a time in our history when good God-fearing people actually (wittingly or unwittingly) have aligned with secular humanists and atheists to fight against God (and his creation) while enshrining and exalting evil! This should be shocking to everyone, and regrettably it is undeniable fact! Since real, justly justice is defined as allowing the equal right to life for all mankind through support and encouragement of the base level of *existence*, we should recognize (for the most part) we have allowed slick justice movements and smooth politicians to manipulate our good intentions and sensibilities while fighting and battling to proliferate base injustices. Even after reading this, I have no doubt that some purportedly good God-fearing and God loving people and politicians will remain united with secular humanists, as they continue the onslaught of assault against "the woman and her offspring." Denials and obfuscations will ensue, but we now have a definitive criterion that will appropriately arm us with the tools to confirm justly justice.

In the pursuit of real justice we are reminded in Romans 1:18-23, that purposely ignoring God leads to a downward spiral. Specifically the scripture reads, "But God's angry displeasure erupts as acts of human mistrust and wrongdoing and lying accumulate, as people try to put a shroud over truth. But the basic reality of God is plain enough. Open your eyes and there it is! By taking a long and thoughtful look at what God has created, people have always been able to see what their eyes as such can't see: eternal power, for instance, and the mystery of his divine being. So nobody has a good excuse. What happened was this: People knew God perfectly well, but when they didn't treat him like God, refusing to worship him, they trivialized themselves into silliness and confusion so that there was neither sense nor direction left in their lives. They pretended to know it all, but were illiterate regarding *life*." (MSSG) . This perfectly encapsulates our predicament, and confirms the importance of this book.

If we can really appreciate this book for what it is, we should see it as a love story. God has enlisted us to fight in an epic battle with and for His divine creation; a creation that culminates with His unceasing love for the "woman and her offspring." If nothing else, this book should help us to better comprehend how precious we are in God's eyes. When we consider God's meticulous care over all creation, His knowing every star by name and His knowing every single hair on each of our heads, it confirms that God has unique plan for each and every infinitesimal aspect of creation. None of it is designed as "throw-away" or is to be rejected! Now, He awaits us!

In this book we confirmed that in our plight we have been duplicitous in our effort toward justice! Surely, we lacked clear definition of the term justice to bring clarity to the issue we "defined and conquered" in the first chapter. Then, we needed to get to the "crux' of the issue in chapter two. After identifying the crux of the matter, we were able to begin confirming whether we will indeed fight based on our "principles or be ruled and governed by "principalities" of our day. As we transitioned further into the read, we were able to discern the "heart of the matter," and we confirmed whether we are "wholly" committed to proliferating injustice, or "Holy" committed to justice. Brutal realities that confirmed the U.S. "ginned" and somehow embraced the worst racist evils in the history of mankind (eugenics) was especially telling, especially since it is still proliferated and embraced today, and accounts for over 60 millions deaths. We noted only "hypocritical oafs" could undergird such brazen injustice. The remedy is "soul food" designed to introspectively nourish our maligned soul and spirit. We began to see it is no longer tenable to ignore the grim realities of "obstructed justice," and took an issue-by-issue look at most of what are considered injustices of our day; in the end, we confirmed most of these issues are permeated by purposeful lies and deceit, but most telling was the realization that all injustice is injustice. The way to solve injustice is to commit to upholding a baseline of justly justice. By the end, we found that if they want to move from the hypocritical "crags to real riches," only a sincere commitment to justly justice can correct the plight of our various justice agencies and politicians.

What we have ultimately discovered is, our current trajectory and predicament has an answer. Importantly, while the problems we face are complex, the answer is narrowed down to a single common denominator. It's "easy," relatively "simplistic," and it can begin to be corrected through simple subtle changes in our capacity to observe and to extend love. In short, the answer is in us. We are the answer! We can begin to correct some of the worst atrocities and human suffering with a minor tweak to our perceptions, a tweak in how we speak about and convey realities, and renewed commitment toward a "righteous" standard of real justly justice.

This book has appropriately deconstructed, refined and confirmed social justice, racial justice and human rights. We should have ever-more zeal and fervent passion about these topics, and we should be compelled in the one direction that promotes existence as a 1st principle for all mankind. This direction is indisputable and beyond reproach;' it is a single message of unification in ensuring justice!

We should now know that the gravity and urgency of this justly justice go well beyond all partisan arguments, devout commitments to Political Parties and ideological recriminations. Expect this renewed justice to propel you beyond the mediocrity and the "typical," beyond frustration and outrage. It should motivate you into prompt action as an unstoppable force that will stand for ALL of the most innocent and least among us!

Real justice is "blind"! This "blindness" should work in two ways. First, it should denote that the scales of justice are evenly weighed without agenda and not skewed to the point of imbalance to ensure an outcome (or agenda). Second, for the purposes of this book, it should denote that each individual should be able to make "blind" choices without consideration to labels, parties, and agendas. Fundamentally we should be able to accommodate the demands of justly justice blindly and without the grip of strongholds that may exist in our soul and spirit.

Dietrich Bonhoeffer confirms, "Silence in the face of evil is itself evil: God will not hold us guiltless. Not to speak is to speak. Not to act is to act." Being silent and not acting here forward is not an option if we are truly committed to real justice. As you now know, this book was not written for cowards! Only the truly principled will be able to make the difference to ensure justly justice for future generations. With the strength of our vote, the power of donations and support, and with word of mouth testimony, we can assure justly justice takes primacy and (going forward) allow us to act with foresight and commitment to our 1st principles. For those who will still attempt to trumpet 'justice," yet hold to evil schemes, they will be confirmed to lack virtue (at best), they become the epitome of a hypocrite, and they must be universally dismissed as liars and shills motivated primarily by selfish political and social gain.

As a final note, a good friend of mine, Walter Hoye, reminded me of Jude 23. The entire book of Jude is quite profound and deserves a serious read and reflection. But verses 18-23 are especially powerful in that they relate directly to the nature of challenge posited in this book; verse 23 is especially poignant as it confirms that there are many in the "fire" that we should help "snatch out of the fire." What's revelatory is that there are many people in the proverbial "fire" and they know it, yet they are not even attempting to escape! In other words, these people are being fully engulfed and consumed by fire, yet they are relishing in it. As we know and fully understand, fire under any circumstances produces pain. Thus these people are willing to endure great suffering and pain, and are not asking for help or reaching out in attempts to escape. With all sensitivity to the relative conundrum of issues presented in this book, Jude helps confirm our plight. We will take our message of real justly justice to the masses, and many will reject it as they relish while being fully consumed by the "flames" of their own traditions/strongholds and lusts. In all love, our response is to help them by "snatching" them out of the fire to escape to ever-consuming flames destined to ruin them.

We must sincerely pray for Godly wisdom about exactly how He would have us "snatch" people out of their complicit destruction. Because this whole effort is fundamentally about His battle, God will assuredly answer. As it relates to this book, "it is finished," but our quest for justly justice has only just begun! Let's redouble our commitment to valiantly fight in in the cosmic battle for God, and do all we can to permanently change the trajectory of America toward a commitment to the 1st principles of justly justice…INDEED!

www.justjustlyjustice.com

ACKNOWLEDGEMENTS

I am especially thankful and grateful to my heavenly Father. Because of His prompting, I was inspired to write this book that confirms His standard for justice. As a direct reflection of His divine inspiration, this entire work was completed in just a couple of weeks! To You, Father, belongs all the glory.

I am also thankful for my family and want to acknowledge my wife Tracey, and our children Sean and Lauren for always supporting and encouraging me to keep "pressing toward the mark of God's high calling."

Special thanks is also extended to the Frederick Douglass Foundation of California (FDFCA). FDFCA is a *real* Justly Just organization committed to ensuring everyone has an opportunity for *life and liberty.* The FDF is tireless in the fight for the equal right to life that culminates with honoring and protecting "...the woman and her offspring," along with all the great Biblical traditions upon which America was founded.

Lastly, I must extend a very special thanks to my good friends Dallas Dellhousaye, Neil Mammen, Jared Duba, Darryl Mueller, Edward Hubbard and Dave Baptist. This book would not have come forth without your commitment and support. I dutifully thank you!

BIBLIOGRAPHY

America's Providential History, Providence Foundation © 1989Mark A. Belilies & Stephen K. McDowell

Ameritopia, Mark R. Levin Copyright © 2012

"And don't call me racist!," Argonaut Press, © 1998 Ella Mazel

C.S. Lewis Society, www.lewissociety.org

Fox News, foxnews.com

Good News Bible, American Bible Society, Good New Translation- Second Edition ©1992

Holy Bible, King James Version, © 1972 Thomas Nelson Inc.

Innovation and Entrepreneurship, Harper & Row Publishers © Peter F. Drucker 1985

Investors Business Daily

Leaders, Harper & Row Publishers, © 1985 Warren Bennis and Burt Nanus

Motherhood in Bondage, 1928,

Newsweek magazine

New York Times

Oxford Concise Dictionary of Politics, © Oxford University Press, Iain McLean and Alistar McMillan- Second edition 2003

Pathway to Leadership, Peace House Publications, Gbile Akanni, © Living Seed Media 2003

Patriot Post, www.patriotpost.us

Scientists Attest to Life Beginning at Conception, Randy Alcorn

The 5000 Year Leap: A Miracle That Changed the World, © 1981 by W. Cleon Skousen, National Center for Constitutional Studies

The Age of Unreason, Harvard Business Schools Press, © 1989 Charles Handy

The Amplified Bible, copyright 1984 , The Lockman Forum

The Bill of Rights Does Not Grant You Any Constitutional Rights, Robert Greenslade & Claude Ellsworth, Nitwit Press

The New Realities, Harper & Row, © Peter Drucker 1989

The Marketing Imagination, Collier Macmillan Publishers, © 1986 Theodore Levitt

The Marketing Of Evil, Cumberland and House Publishing, Inc. © 2005 David Kupelian

The Message Bible, Navipress, © 1995 Eugene H. Patterson

The Story of The Constitution, House Office Publishing, © 1937 Sol Bloom

The Pivot of Civilization, 1922,

USA TODAY

Wall Street Journal

World Magazine and WorldMag (www.worldmag.com)

World News Digest (WND.com)

Made in the USA
San Bernardino, CA
06 April 2016